THE DAY THE

Laughter

Died

VOLUME 1:
VAUDEVILLE THRU THE 1950s

Catherine F. Olen

The Day the Laughter Died
Volume I: Vaudeville through the 1950s

© 2021 Catherine Olen

First paperback edition May 2021

ISBN 978-1-64822-018-0 (paperback)
ISBN 978-1-64822-019-7 (eBook)

Published by Catherine F. Olen
www.Mousehangover.com
Cover art by Christian Lange
Caricature art by Sheldon Moonjelil

Readers are welcome to contact the publisher for comments, updates, or questions.

Disclaimer

Trademarks: This book contains copy-righted characters, registered trademarks, marks, and registered marks. All references to these properties are made solely for editorial purposes.

Neither the author nor the publisher makes any commercial claim to their use, and neither is affiliated with the entities or film properties. All references to these properties are made solely for editorial purposes. Neither the author nor the publisher makes any commercial claims to their use, and neither is affiliated to these works or the producing entities.

About the Author

Catherine Olen has spent many years working in and around cemeteries. In her early years, she worked as a family service counselor at several Southern California mortuaries. During this time, she began searching and visiting the final resting places of many of Hollywood's biggest stars. What began as a hobby grew quickly into a career with the creation of Hollywood Grave Hunter.

The HollywoodGraveHunter.com website that she created has become a huge success. Catherine has been featured on Entertainment Tonight, Reelz, Biography Channel, and the Mark and Brian radio show giving her audience her unique view into the lives and deaths of their favorite celebrities.

With all that to occupy her time, somehow, she found the time put down here the funniest, strangest, and most outlandish experiences and stories she's come across during two decades of researching the lives of Hollywood's A-list celebrities. Catherine currently resides in Los Angeles, California, with her family and continues working on her writing passion.

Come Check Us Out

www.HollywoodGraveHunter.com
@ Hollywoodgravehunter – Facebook
Other books by Catherine Olen:
The Day the Laughter Died
The Final Curtain: Celebrity Deaths

Dedication

To everyone who gave me their support and assistance in the process of finishing this book

To Every person that has fallen in love with film throughout the years

Lastly, my thanks to the artists for the vision that created these amazing movies

Table of Contents

Introduction

When I started to write this book, I was going through a rough period in my life. Health, marriage, family, and financial problems plagued every corner of my life. I finished working one evening after a particularly bad day and asked my daughter to pick out a movie for us to watch. I was in a rotten mood and knew I did not want to go out or interact with anyone; I just wanted to be still and forget for a while.

"What kind of movie do you want?" she asked

"Comedy" was my response. The need to shut down and laugh was overwhelming.

She came back into the room and handed me a film *Sneakers* made in 1992, starring Robert Redford, Dan Aykroyd, Sidney Poitier, River Phoenix, and Sir Ben Kingsley. We shared this film together for the next two hours, laughing at the jokes and situations we found the character in. The day's events, stress, and frustration seemed to evaporate, and I felt better when the final credits began to roll. I could smile more easily than when I left my desk and felt like myself again.

What is it about comedy that holds so many of us captive? Researchers and psychologists have theorized that laughter is a fundamental part of everyday life. In the

November 1, 2000 issue of *Psychology Today*, the writer suggests " laughter is primarily a social vocalization that binds people together. It is a hidden language that we all speak. It is not a learned group reaction but an instinctive behavior programmed by our genes. Laughter bonds us through humor and play."

As we watch a movie or television show, we laugh at the same pratfalls and gags we have seen hundreds of times. These comedy standards always seem to get the same response, whether seen for the first time or in reruns. We laugh alone, but more often, in a group of friends, indicating the pleasure we find in humor intensifies during social situations.

Comedy has been a part of culture dating back to the ancient Greek and Roman eras. The ability to laugh is distinctly human, and people have been entertaining audiences for millennia. The art of comedy is designed to exaggerate normal behaviors with speech or action in a light-hearted way to amuse and entertain the audience. In Roman culture, the comedy would play out in the family situation with a mother, father, and son acting out a scene where the father and son were in love with the same girl, with the father having to face his irate wife at the end of the play and the son bumbling his way through the courtship to win the girl of his dreams. Secondary characters would play minor roles but were strategically placed through the story to move the plot along or garner additional chuckles from the audience. In all of these plays, the names and faces may have changed, but the formula to make people laugh remained constant.

At the turn of the twentieth century, Vaudeville became the standard for comedy, with performers working on-stage juggling furiously, dancing, or taking a fall to the reward of uproarious laughter from the crowd. Troupes of performers would travel across the United States, entertaining the masses. However, this way of life for entertainers was threatened when a new invention by Thomas Edison called the Magic Lantern. This new invention would show people and animals moving on a screen. This new entertainment soon became the rage across the country and these national superstars of the stage needed to reinvent themselves to stay in the public eye.

The advent of comedy in film dates back to 1895, when the first crude images were displayed frame by frame in nickelodeons. One of the first comedies was entitled *Sneeze* by Fred Ott. This five-second film shows Ott, assistant to Thomas Edison, taking a pinch of snuff and sneezing. A simple premise eliciting giggles from the patrons. Many of Vaudeville's top performers found their way to the movie studios reinventing many of their stage acts on film for a broader audience.

Throughout the generations, comedy has become more sophisticated or crude, depending on the audience's tastes. But one thing remains true, comedy in films and television will be a constant with studios looking for new, innovative ways to make us laugh.

We laugh on cue at appropriate moments during a movie. We find a pie in the face or fall into a swimming pool universally humorous. We idolize the men and women who make us laugh, rushing to the comedy club to watch a stand-up routine or going to the theater to watch the latest movie starring Adam Sandler, Robin Williams, or Eddie Murphy. The acclaim of comedy has even gone so far as to make animated characters like Bugs Bunny and Daffy Duck international superstars. Generations have made the cartoons of the 1930s and 1940s just as popular today as during their original theatrical release.

The men and women of comedy, with that intangible knack for humor that, keep us entertained. That certain something that cannot be learned is reflected back to the stage with people doubled over laughing until tears form in the corner of their eyes. Comedy great Rodney Dangerfield certainly got more respect on stage than he claimed to get offstage. The original cast of *Saturday Night Live* became comedy royalty, with Chevy Chase, Dan Akyroyd, John Belushi, Gilda Radner, and Eddie Murphy making their mark on comedy's history.

As the end of the 20th century approached, new stars came to the public eye. *The Simpsons* have become one of the longest-running animated series in history. *South Park* and *Family Guy* brought a new assault on the senses with varying degrees of adult situations and vulgarity peppering the comedic undertones.

Whatever your style of comedy, the film will continue to make us laugh, and the stars on the screen will be lifted upon the pedestals for us to adore with our laughter.

Vaudeville paves the way for film 1910 - 1930

As our country welcomed the twentieth century, the entertainment industry was set in its ways, with theaters nationwide showing Vaudeville acts entertaining people from every corner of the country. Little did the theater owners or performers realize that there would be an invention that would revolutionize entertainment and shake their world to its foundation.

Moving pictures began as simple images flickering across the screen in nickelodeons. The films were crude and the entertainers unsophisticated, but the audiences flocked to see the same films repeatedly. Suddenly, theaters across the country were retrofitting their theaters with these nickelodeon machines and the live acts were finding it harder to get work. Dancers, singers, comedians, and acrobats fought for their lives while traditional theaters were becoming scarce. The smart ones found their way to the studios as they were hungry for new talent, churning out hundreds of short films a month. Those who clung to their stage careers soon found themselves on the street or looking for work in factories.

The comedians of the stage were the new movie stars on the screen. Since early films were silent, the story had to be communicated to the audience through movement, and who better to do this than the men and women who had been making people laugh on the stage. Actors like Billy West, Edna Purviance, Mack Swain, and Harry Langdon would never become movie stars, but they maintained a faithful audience that kept them working steadily. It was that lucky few like Charlie Chaplin and John Bunny that eventually would become major motion picture stars and engrave their names on the history of the early comedy films.

Harold Lloyd

Known throughout the world as one of the greatest comedians of the silent film era, Harold Lloyd garnered the label of the highest-paid actor of the 1920s, becoming one of the first superstars of silent movies. No one would have ever guessed he would become an icon to be immortalized forever on the silver screen based on his meager beginnings.

Harold Lloyd was born in Buchard, Nebraska, to Elizabeth Fraser and J. Darcie 'Foxy' Lloyd. It was not a happy marriage as Lloyd's father fought to divorce his overbearing mother. At the turn of the century, this was unheard of and created quite the scandal for the Lloyd family. Harold moved with his father to San Diego, California, and continued his education there, eventually training at the San Diego School of Dramatic Art.

Lloyd's father struggled financially but, in 1913, received a generous settlement from a previous accident, and this allowed the two male Lloyd's to move west. Once the younger Lloyd arrived in Southern California, he opened a pool hall which quickly went under due to his poor management skills. Lloyd's father recommended he audition for a movie being made locally with San Diego's Pan American Exposition by the Edison Company. On the set of this movie, Lloyd was first introduced to the man that would influence his career like no other, Hal Roach. He and Roach would part ways after this first film, but not for long.

In 1915, Lloyd began working at Universal Studios under the great director Mack Sennett's direction, known as the king of the comedies. Lloyd appeared in several shorts films with the Keystone comedy troupe under Sennett's constant supervision.

Later that same year, Hal Roach opened his studio, Phun Philms, which he quickly renamed Rolin Studios. Roach produced two-reel comedies, and Lloyd's character, at first, was a cheap version of the Charlie Chaplin little tramp character that was so well known. In 1917, the two men decided to dump the character, and Lloyd adopted his every man with glasses persona, which was inspired by the Clark Kent Superman character. Roach released up to three new films each month starring Lloyd, and the audience approval was staggering.

In 1919, while working with a prop bomb on set, the device went off accidentally, and Lloyd lost his right thumb and forefinger in the accident. Lloyd would go to great lengths to hide this deformity, having prosthetic gloves made or hiding his hand when he was photographed. This went on long after he retired from show business.

Even with all of this fame and success during their partnership, Lloyd had decided early that working with someone else was not going to be a long-term proposition.

In 1925, Lloyd moved to Paramount studios and began working on his own films. One of his first costars was the lovely Bebe Daniels, and the two fell in love. Unfortunately, Daniels learned quickly that Lloyd would not commit to a long-term relationship, and the two parted ways amicably. Lloyd would eventually marry costar Mildred Davis in 1925, and the two had three children together. Mildred retired from acting to raise their family in the thirty-two-room mansion Lloyd built for her over the course of three years.

During the 1920s, Lloyd's success seemed unstoppable. He earned 1.5 million dollars per picture while working with Paramount Studios.

In 1928, Lloyd shot his last silent film *Speedy* in New York City. With the advent of sound, the studio quickly changed the format, but Lloyd became nervous at the prospect of sound films. His films were solely based on physical comedy, and he fretted about how the sound format would affect the final product.

In 1929, Lloyd starred in his first talking picture, and by all accounts, it was a total failure critically but went on to gross over three million dollars. His next two sound films were critical and financial disasters, and Lloyd's career began a freefall from which he never recovered.

By 1934, Lloyd's films were dying at the box office. Lloyd moved on to Fox Studios for *The Cat's Paw*, another flop. Lloyd went back to Paramount for a two-picture deal, but both films lost money, and the studio insisted that any further films would need a personal guarantee financially from Lloyd. At the age of forty-five, Harold Lloyd's career was over. Lloyd left the film industry a commercial failure but a very wealthy man from his varied investments through the years.

While he missed working, Lloyd busied himself with his family and many hobbies, including photography, collecting cars, and high-fidelity stereo systems. It was rumored that Lloyd was a womanizer, leaving a string of illegitimate children in his wake. While this rumor persisted, no one came forward to claim rights to his vast fortune.

In 1941, Lloyd tried his hand once more at film making, becoming a producer of two pictures at RKO studios. Once again, the films failed to bring a profit, and this was the final nail in the coffin for Lloyd's professional career.

Lloyd immersed himself in photography and amassed over two hundred and fifty thousand images over the course of thirty years. Several hundred of the images featuring starlets in the nude.

His wife Mildred passed away in 1951 after a long bout with alcoholism. The couple was married for forty-six years, and Mildred was known for her lavish Hollywood parties and her love for her numerous friends.

After her death, Harold threw himself into good works for the city of Los Angeles. He was a member of the Shriner's® organization and devoted his time to the Shriner's® hospital for disabled children.

In 1952, Lloyd received a lifetime Academy Award®; it was said at the presentation that he was a "master comedian and a good citizen."

In 1962, he compiled some of his silent comedies into two documentaries called *Harold Lloyd's World of Comedy* & *Harold Lloyd's Funny Side of Life*.

Lloyd was diagnosed with prostate cancer by his brother in law Jack Davis, who was his family physician. He died March 8, 1971, at his home, surrounded by his family.

On Thursday, March 11, 1971, a funeral service was held for Lloyd at the Scottish Rite Temple in Los Angeles, California. Over one thousand people were in attendance, including Milton Berle, Red Skelton, Jack Warner, and Buddy Rogers. George M. Saunders of the Shriner's® hospital for disabled children gave the eulogy. The pallbearers who carried Lloyd's casket to its final resting place were all members of the Shriner's® organization. His body was laid to rest in the Great Mausoleum at Forest Lawn Memorial Park in Glendale, California.

Charlie Chaplin

The diminutive little tramp with baggy pants, derby hat, and oversized shoes is one of the best-loved characters in film history. Charlie Chaplin, the man who changed the face of film, epitomized the man who was struggling through life but continued to entertain, no matter the trials he endured.

When asked about his childhood, Chaplin simply stated that anything people wanted to know about his life could be discovered through his films.

Charles Spencer Chaplin was born to Charles and Hannah Chaplin, who worked as dance hall performers in London, England. Chaplin claimed he was born in Fountainbleu, France, but this was a fabrication woven by either his mother or Chaplin himself. Born on East Street in London, he lived with his mother, father, and older brother Sidney. The family moved to West Square when he was very young. His father was a very successful stage performer but drank to excess daily, causing problems with his stage act. By 1891, Charles Sr moved in with friends, leaving Hannah to raise the boys alone.

Over the next few years, his mother performed on the stage while raising her boys in a nice little home until she remarried. Hannah gave birth to another son, Leo Dryden, but the boy was taken by his father at the age of 6 months. The Chaplin's would not see the boy again for thirty years.

Hannah left the stage, became a nurse and dressmaker to make ends meet for her small family. She attempted to revive her stage career but froze on-stage one night with Chaplin watching from the wings. She was booed by the spectators and hit with rotten vegetables. Chaplin rushed to the stage and began singing and dancing for the unruly audience. He enchanted the crowd, who enthusiastically cheered for him.

At the age of six, Chaplin and his mother were separated. Hannah was admitted to Lamberth infirmary Workhouse, and, as a result of her illness, Chaplin was sent to live with relatives. However, his brother Sidney was sent to a school outside of London, which further tore them apart. Hannah recovered briefly from her ailment, and the boys reunited with their mother, but she was readmitted to the hospital within a year.

The boys found themselves in and out of poor children's homes over the next few years as Hannah struggled with her mental and physical health. These workhouses and homes were known for their brutality towards the children and poverty level living conditions, and the boys suffered greatly at the hands of their caregivers.

By the time he was ten years old, Chaplin had begun clog dancing on the stage. He took odd jobs to help his family financially, and his brother Sidney had gone to sea, working for many years on the trade ships. Even with his mother's failing mental health, he loved her dearly and would continue to support her for the rest of her life.

Chaplin won a role in the tour company of *Sherlock Holmes* and maintained steady work on the stage. He reunited with his brother, and the two men worked together, touring with various plays. At the turn of the twentieth century, the two brothers had become affluent and lived a rich life in London along with their mother. In 1919, the touring company sent players to the United States to perform, and Chaplin was selected to go. One of his fellow performers was a young Stan Jefferson, who would later go on to be one of the biggest names in silent film as Stan Laurel.

Chaplin's drunk character was well received by American audiences. The touring company returned to London, but Chaplin knew that this new land was to eventually be his home and vowed to return.

On October 2, 1912, Chaplin boarded a ship for America, knowing his new life was just beginning. He decided this was to be his home for the rest of his life, or so he thought. Over the next year, Chaplin worked on the stage, but the film industry, still in its infancy, was growing steadily. He was discovered by director Mack Sennett of the Keystone Film studio and was offered a contract to perform in short subject films. In December 1913, Chaplin arrived on the Keystone set. His first film, *Making a Living,* was directed by Henry Lehrman. Lehrman and Chaplin clashed on the direction of the film, and eventually, all Chaplin's jokes and improvisation were removed from the final film causing Chaplin to hate the final product.

His next film, *Kid's Auto Races,* introduced his little tramp character that would be his trademark for the rest of his career. He wore baggy pants, an undersized jacket, and oversized shoes worn on the wrong feet to keep from falling off. The toothbrush mustache and cane completed the look, and the little tramp was born.

Even with his enormous success with Keystone, Chaplin was not happy. Feeling he knew what would work best on film, Chaplin harassed the studio powers to allow him to direct his own films. Keystone studio finally decided to let him have his way and direct himself. This decision to let Chaplin direct resulted in many successful films.

At the end of Chaplin's contract with Keystone studio, most of the big movie studios attempted to woo him away with offers of large sums of money, but it was the First National films that offered Chaplin the brass ring of one million dollars for eight films. He took the offer, completed the contract, and then moved on to open his own studio, ensuring he would maintain complete creative control over his films. In 1919, he in addition to Douglas Fairbanks, Mary Pickford, and D.W. Griffith formed United Artists.

While professionally Chaplin was on top of the world, personally he struggled to find a woman to share his life with. In 1918, Chaplin met actress Mildred

Harris, and the two began having an affair. Harris came to Chaplin claiming to be pregnant, and the two were wed immediately to avoid any scandal in the newspapers. After the two married, Chaplin found out the pregnancy was a false alarm, but it was too late. Mildred and her mother moved into Chaplin's palatial estate, and this is where his real troubles began. The two had nothing in common, and Chaplin's mother-in-law attempted to rule their home. The couple did have one son together, Norman Spencer Chaplin, but the child only lived three days. Chaplin divorced Harris in 1920, and the divorce was very ugly and very public, with Mildred and her mother attempting to get their hands on Chaplin's latest film, *The Kid*. Chaplin fled the state and managed to keep his film from being seized in the divorce. The divorce cost Chaplin a small fortune, and his name was dragged through the mud during the proceedings, but he managed to come out of it with his career still intact.

Chaplin was linked romantically with several actresses of the time but managed to stay clear of any further scandal. In 1924, Chaplin met actress Lita Grey on the set of the film *The Gold Rush*. Learning nothing from his past, he found himself with another pregnant bride and an overbearing mother-in-law. The couple had two sons together, but Chaplin was miserable in the marriage and wanted nothing more but to remove himself from the situation. In 1927, Chaplin was involved in another expensive divorce, and Grey walked away with three thousand dollars a month in spousal support.

Many changes were taking place in Chaplin's life, the least of which was the invention of talking pictures.

Talking pictures began to dominate the cinema, but Chaplin felt that the magic would be gone if the Little Tramp spoke. He released his next film, *City Lights,* to great success despite the competition of talking films.

In June 1932, Chaplin met actress Paulette Godard, the two courted and eventually married. The couple stayed married until 1942 and parted ways, staying close for many years. The two appeared in *Modern Times*, another silent film that gained great success.

In 1943, Chaplin appeared in his first talking film, *The Great Dictator,* a comic parody of Adolf Hitler and the Third Reich. A dangerous undertaking, the film was a monumental success with audiences, but the government felt the subject matter was in poor taste and began questioning Chaplin's patriotism to the United States. Chaplin found himself being attacked by several groups within the U.S., and his fame took a turn for the worse, with audiences believing the headline about Chaplin's unamerican beliefs.

It was during this time that Chaplin met the daughter of the famous playwriter Eugene O'Neill. Oona O'Neill was only eighteen years old when the two met, but Chaplin fell madly in love with the dark-haired beauty, and the two were married. Chaplin was captivated by Oona's serenity and proved to be a perfect fit for Chaplin's life. Oona supported her husband's career above her own and let her film career slip away to focus on the marriage. Chaplin was being accused of anti-American activities during the early years of their marriage, but this did little to diminish the happiness he felt with his new found wife.

The Chaplin family grew with eight more children, giving him eleven children throughout his four marriages.

In 1952, Chaplin and his family traveled to England for the premiere of his film *Limelight*. Chaplin had never filed for citizenship in the United States, and the government had the perfect opportunity to get rid of the man who had charmed audiences for decades. It was not until the ship sailed out of New York harbor that Chaplin was notified that he would not be allowed back into the U.S. as his re-entry permit had been canceled subject to an investigation into his life and work.

The family settled in Switzerland, and Oona Chaplin gave up her U.S. citizenship to live out her days with her husband. Their family continued to be happy and successful surrounded by their children.

Chaplin did not return to the U.S. until 1972 to receive a special Oscar® for his contribution to the film industry. Chaplin came back to the country that had scorned him so viciously to attend the awards show, insisting that *The Great Dictator* be included in a film montage of his life's work. Chaplin told producers that if this film was not included, he would not be attending. The Academy granted his request, and the little tramp was finally given the admiration he deserved from his fellow artists.

In 1975, Chaplin was knighted by the queen of England, making him Sir Charles Chaplin. While the accolade of his life came late, they were well-received nonetheless.

It was Christmas day of 1977 that Charles Chaplin died, surrounded by family in his home in Switzerland. A lengthy obituary was written by Bosley Crowther for the Los Angeles Times; below is a small part of the tribute:

Charlie Chaplin, the poignant little tramp with the cane and comic walk who almost single-handedly elevated the novelty entertainment medium of motion pictures into art, died peacefully yesterday at his home in Switzerland. He was 88 years old.

Sir Charles -- he was knighted by Queen Elizabeth in 1975 -- died at 4 A.M., a few hours before his family's traditional Christmas celebration was to begin.

His wife, Oona, daughter of the playwright Eugene O'Neill, and seven of their children were at the bedside when the comedian died. A daughter, the actress Geraldine Chaplin, was in Madrid making a film, but left immediately to join her family at the Chaplin home at Corsiersur-Vevey, a village near the eastern tip of the Lake of Geneva.

"All the presents were under the tree," Lady Chaplin told a caller, adding, "Charlie gave so much happiness and, although he had been ill for a long time, it is so sad that he should have passed away on Christmas day."

"He died of old age," said Dr. Henri Perrier, the Chaplin family physician. "His death was peaceful and calm." A source close to the family said Sir Charles had been given oxygen because of breathing trouble in recent days.

In a statement, Lady Chaplin said the funeral would be private and restricted to the immediate family. A family spokesman said the funeral might be held in England but that burial would probably be in Switzerland, Sir Charles's home since his self-imposed exile from the United States in 1952.

Sir Charles had been in failing health for many years. He was confined to a wheelchair and his speech, hearing and sight were impaired. During the last year, he left his secluded 20-room villa only for an occasional drive into Vevey with his wife. Local people caught an occasional glimpse of the famous actor waiting in his blue-and-silver Rolls- Royce while his *wife, 35 year his junior, purchased English newspapers and magazines, which she read to him later.*

His last public appearance took place last fall when he attended a circus performance in Vevey. He wore a soft hat pulled down over his forehead and thick-lensed glasses that hid most of his face. He shook hands with one of the clowns at the end of the performance.

No motion picture actor so captured and enthralled the world as did Charles Spencer Chaplin, a London ragamuffin who became an immortal artist for his deft and effective humanization of man's tragicomic conflicts with fate. In more than 80 movies from 1914 to 1967, he either portrayed or elaborated (he was a writer and director as well as an actor) the theme of the little fellow capriciously knocked about by life, but not so utterly battered that he did not pick himself up in the hope that the next encounter would turn out better.

Chaplin was laid to rest in Corsier-Sur-Vevey, Switzerland, in a private family funeral. Unfortunately, this is not where the story of the great Charlie Chaplin ends. On March 1, 1978, two months after his death, a group of local mechanics exhumed the remains of the prodigious comedian and attempted to extort money from the Chaplin family. The plan failed, as the thieves could not stay quiet about the crime, and they were brought to justice. Chaplin's body was found eleven weeks later and was reburied under six feet of concrete to ensure no further grave robbing attempts would be made.

Oona Chaplin died on September 27, 1991, and she was laid to rest next to her beloved husband of thirty-six years.

Laurel & Hardy

One of the most famous comedy duos in the history of motion pictures, Stan Laurel and Oliver Hardy, seemed to be destined for greatness, even when it seemed they would never work together on film.

Stan Laurel

Stan Laurel was born into a theatrical family, his father an actor and theater manager. At the age of sixteen, Arthur Stanley Jefferson first step on the stage at Pickard's Museum in Glasgow, England. Soon after his debut, Laurel joined Fred Karno's troupe of performers with another unknown by the name of Charles Chaplin. The troupe performed with Chaplin as one of the premier players, and Laurel was cast as his understudy for many performances. In 1910, the troupe came to the United States to great success and returned in 1913 to rave reviews.

In 1917 that Stan Laurel decided to move to the United States permanently after being cast in a two-reel comedy *Nuts in May*. Laurel worked steadily with several movie studios, including Metro Goldwyn Mayer, Hal Roach Studios, and Universal Pictures, in the early years of his career.

In 1926, Laurel decided to shift the focus of his career to writing and directing. In that same year, he was introduced to another popular comedy actor, Oliver Hardy. The two were cast in the 1926 film *45 Minutes from Hollywood,* starring screen vamp Theda Bara. This would be the last film Laurel would commit to until 1927, although he continued living in Los Angeles during his hiatus. When Oliver Hardy was injured during the filming of his latest short subject film, the director asked Stan Laurel to step in, and he agreed to assist with the completion of the film. Once again, Laurel began work again, completing the film *Seeing the World* costarring with the Our Gang kids. After his recovery, Hardy was partnered with Laurel in the films *Duck Soup* and *Slipping Wives.*

Oliver Hardy

Oliver Hardy was born Norvell Hardy, the youngest of five children, to a Scottish-English family on January 18, 1892. Hardy was known as an incorrigible child and was sent to Milledgeville military academy at a very young age.

Hardy had little interest in school but excelled at theater and music. By the age of eight, Hardy was a gifted singer and enjoyed performing for his school friends. Hardy ran away from a boarding school in Atlanta, Georgia, to join a troupe of performers determined to be a performer at any cost. His mother encouraged his singing and paid for a tutor, but Hardy would not show up for lessons. Instead, he performed at the local Alcatraz theater for $3.50 a week. At this time, Hardy added the name Oliver to his moniker, a tribute to his father, who died when Hardy was only a year old. This singing career would be short-lived, and Hardy would end up back in Milledgeville with his family by 1910.

It was this same year that Hardy took a job with the local theater. He worked as a projectionist, ticket taker, janitor, and manager. During his tenure at the theater, Hardy became obsessed with the new moving pictures replacing the live acts. In 1913, Hardy decided he could do better than the faces on the screen and moved to Jacksonville, Florida, where several movie companies have set up studios. The next year, Hardy would make his first film *Outwitting Dad.* The six-foot one-inch hardy weighed in at almost three hundred pounds but was billed as "Babe Hardy." By the end of 1915, Hardy had made over fifty-one reel films for Lubin studios in Florida and decided to move to New York to work with Pathe studios. Hardy worked steadily between New York and Florida until 1917 when he moved to Hollywood and began working as a freelance with several movie studios on the west coast. He worked with Vitagraph and Hal Roach studios, playing the tin man in the 1925 production of *The Wizard of Oz* starring Dorothy Dwan.

In 1924, Hardy was cast in the film *Yes, Yes, Nanette!*, directed by Stan Laurel. The two worked well together as actor and director, but the two parted ways without a second glance once the filming was over. Fate would step in, though, as Hardy was cast in the film *Get 'em Young* and was burned by a hot leg of lamb. Stan Laurel was asked to step in to finish the film for the injured actor.

The two men were cast in the film 45 *Minutes from Hollywood* but never shared any scenes in the film. Two other films came quickly after, *Duck Soup* and *With Love and Hisse*s, with Laurel and Hardy working together briefly on film in a few scenes. The studio watched the audience's reaction to the duo and intentionally paired the two men together in a series of films from 1929 through 1932. Their film *The Music Box* won an Academy Award® that same year for Best Short Film.

In 1940, the pair made the films *A Chump at Oxford* and *Saps at Sea* before committing to the USO to perform for the troupes during World War II. Laurel and Hardy continued working steadily throughout the 1940s with Hal Roach Studios and Twentieth Century Fox and MGM Studios.

In 1947, the team toured Great Britain with some reservations about their popularity abroad but found they were mobbed everywhere they visited. With the huge success abroad, the tour was extended to include Scandinavia, Belgium, and France, including a command performance for King George VI and Queen Elizabeth.

In 1950, Laurel and Hardy would make their final film together, *Utopia,* about two men traveling to their private island who wind up stranded on an atoll and setting up their own government along with their fellow castaways. A team of international investors funded the film. The cast was made up of actors speaking various languages, made of difficulties on the set since the cast could not understand the director. This, paired with both Laurel and Hardy's physical illnesses, made for long and difficult filming. The pair retired from films but was offered a series of television programs based on the Mother Goose fables in 1955. Unfortunately, this series was never realized as Laurel suffered a debilitating stroke that year, and Hardy suffered both a stroke and heart attack the next year.

The two men would be plagued with incapacitating health for the rest of their lives. Hardy lost over one hundred and fifty pounds over the next two years. Some suspected that he had cancer, but nothing was ever brought to the public to confirm or deny this. After a serious stroke on September 14, 1954, Hardy was bedridden and unable to speak for months. Laurel visited Hardy often, the two not speaking but communicating through facial expressions, a talent brought on from years of silent film acting.

In early August 1957, the great comedian suffered two more strokes leaving him in a coma from which he never awoke.

Oliver Hardy died on August 7, 1957, at the age of sixty-five. The death certificate read a laundry list of contributing causes to his death. Laurel was devastated upon hearing of his old friends' death and refused to attend the funeral stating, "Babe would understand."

The Los Angeles Times obituary was a tribute to the famous comedian:

Oliver Hardy, rotund film comedian, died yesterday.

He was 65.

Death came to the portly half of the famed Laurel and Hardy comedy team from the effects of a paralytic stroke he suffered last Sept. 12. So severe was the stroke that it left him almost completely paralyzed. He was unable to speak and could hardly move one arm. He wasted away to a comparative shadow from his comical bumbling bulk which at the height of his fame bulged to 350 pounds.

At his bedside when Hardy died was his wife, Mrs. Virginia Lucille Hardy, whom he wed 17 years ago when she was a studio script girl. Death occurred at the home of Hardy's mother-in-law, Mrs. Monnie L. Jones, 5421 Auckland St., North

> *Hollywood, where the comedian and his wife had been living for the last six months.*
>
> *"It was a blessing for him," said Mrs. Hardy. "He is finally out of his suffering and he did not suffer at the end. After that stroke 11 months ago, Oliver had another Sunday, and a third yesterday which sent him into a coma. He never emerged from it. His heart just stopped beating."*

After a private funeral, Hardy was cremated and buried at Valhalla Memorial Park in Los Angeles, California. A large bronze plaque adorns the urn garden above his burial space, stating, "A Genius of Comedy. His talent brought joy and laughter to all the world."

After Hardy's death, Laurel never made another personal appearance. He died at his home in Santa Monica, California, on February 23, 1965, surrounded by his family.

It is rumored that Laurel stated to his nurse the day of his death, "I wish I were skiing right now."

The nurse replied, " I didn't know you skied." To which he replied, "I don't, but it is better than what I am doing now." These were his last words; he died within minutes of the exchange.

The Desert Sun printed a tribute to the comedian on February 24, 1965:

> *STAN LAUREL DIES AT 74 Harmless Little Man Who Couldn't Win; He'll Be Remembered*
>
> *SANTA MONICA, Calif. (UPI) —Millions will never forget him because he was one of them — the little man. the harmless*

chap who never succeeds no matter how hard he tries. That was the story of Stan Laurel's life in the movies the easy going fellow who always seems to get knocked about by the big man. The big man, in Laurel's case, of course was his partner, fat Oliver (Babe) Hardy. Their partnership ended after a 30-year association in 1957 when Hardy died following a stroke. Broken-hearted Stan Laurel never again appeared in public. Tuesday Laurel died after a heart attack at the age of 74. The thin-rubber-faced comedian's fourth wife, Ida, was with him when he was stricken in their modest home here. Laurel had been partially paralyzed since 1955, when he, too. suffered a stroke. In recent years, he also was afflicted by diabetes. Laurel and Hardy were the, most successful comedy team in movie history.

The funeral for Stan Laurel was held at Forest Lawn Memorial Park in Hollywood Hills. Dick Van Dyke gave a tearful eulogy while fellow comedian Buster Keaton was rumored to state, "Chaplin wasn't the funniest, I wasn't the funniest, this man was the funniest." Other films comedy greats the likes of Patsy Kelly, Joe Flynn, and Tim Conway, were in attendance along with Hal Roach, Jr., Pat Buttram, and Alan Mowbray all attended the funeral to pay their respects to the great man.

Laurel was cremated and buried at Forest Lawn Memorial Park in the Hollywood Hills. A plaque similar to the one erected to his friend adorns the gravesite wall just above where the comedian was laid to rest. "A Master of Comedy. His genius in the art of humor brought gladness to the world he loved."

Buster Keaton

Known as "The Great Stone Face," Buster Keaton is one of the best-known silent film actors and is considered a master of physical comedy. With his deadpan face, pork pie hat, and bow tie, Keaton became an icon of silent comedy films. To this day, Keaton is revered as the inspiration of great comedians, including John Ritter, Jim Carey, and Harvey Korman.

Buster Keaton was born into a Vaudeville family from Piqua, Kansas, on October 4, 1895. Named Joesph at birth, Keaton was the sixth Joseph in the Keaton family, upholding a long tradition of namesakes for each generation.

Appearing on stage at a very early age Keaton, along with his parents, performed an act centered around a child who was in desperate need of discipline. Keaton would be thrown around the stage and into the audience, always with a deadpan look on his face throughout the scene. The family taught Keaton how to fall so he would not be injured, but on several occasions, the police were called in to investigate claims of child abuse after the rough and tumble shows. The young Keaton learned quickly every aspect of physical comedy, which became his signature style throughout his career. Keaton learned to sing, dance, juggle, perform magic tricks and play the piano while a youngster and honed his craft backstage while his family performed in theaters across the country. He would later use all of these skills to create his act on the stage and later in his films.

Keaton continued performing with his family well into his teen years. It was his father's alcoholism that eventually threatened the family act, so Keaton and his mother moved to New York to salvage their careers, leaving his father on his own.

While in New York, Keaton began acting in the new medium of film. While he had reservations about the new invention at first, Keaton found freedom on film that could not be captured on the stage and soon adapted very well to motion pictures. Keaton's first film, *The Butcher Boy,* found him performing opposite well-known comedian Roscoe Arbuckle. The two became good friends, with Arbuckle eventually allowing Keaton to direct him and write all of his gags. It was not until 1920 that Keaton was cast in his first starring role in the picture *The Saphead.* With the success of Keaton's films with Talmadge studio's, Keaton was given his own production unit, Buster Keaton Comedies, under producer Joseph Schenck's tutelage. From 1920 to 1922, Keaton produced two-reel featurettes to boundless success, and he was given the green light to begin making full-length feature films by the studio.

Keaton used the camera much differently than other directors at the time. Keaton was able to incorporate subtleties with wit and satire in his films, unseen by other filmmakers. His use of dark elements, along with heart-touching drama, created magic on the screen.

In addition to performing in all of his films, Keaton also performed all of his own stunts. On the set of the film, *Sherlock Jr.* Keaton broke his neck as he fell from a water tank and landed on a stretch of railroad tracks. It was not until years later that he realized the extent of his injury and sought help to repair his neck. Many times, the audience was oblivious to the extreme danger of the scenes caught on film. In the iconic film *Steamboat Bill Jr.* Keaton was required to run into the scene and stop at an exact spot on the set while a building fell around him. Only a window no large than his body left the actor from being crushed by the falling structure. The scene was pulled off with perfect timing and is known as one of the greatest stunts ever to be caught on film.

Keaton's most famous film, *The General,* was based on a true story about civil war northern spies who steal a Confederate train with Keaton playing the engineer in the film.

In 1928, Keaton signed with MGM studios against his better judgment and the advice of friends like Charlie Chaplin and Harold Lloyd. He made several successful sound pictures with the studio, although he lost creative control and stopped directing. Keaton continued to keep audiences laughing with his creative on-screen antics but felt impaired creatively. In 1932, MGM paired Keaton with comedy giant Jimmy Durante for a series of films, including *The Passionate Plumber* and *What! No Beer?*

After he was released from his contract with MGM, Keaton appeared in a series of educational films then expanded his performances to include internationally produced films. Keaton would also begin writing again for up-and-coming comedians like Red Skelton and Lucille Ball. In the late 1940s, Keaton rediscovered his love of acting and was brought back to star in motion pictures. Friend Ed Wynn invited Keaton to appear on his new television show, *The Ed Wynn Show.* Keaton agreed and found a whole new generation of viewers to introduce to his comedy.

In 1950, Keaton starred in his own television show *The Buster Keaton Show,* a live series that gave Keaton the opportunity to recreate his classic comedy sketches for the burgeoning television audience. Keaton was uncomfortable with the demand of a weekly starring role and felt he could not keep up with the need for fresh material each week, which doomed the show to a short run. Keaton continued working in television with guest appearances on hit shows like *The Donna Reed Show* and *The Twilight Zone*.

In the 1960s, Keaton, now in his seventies, worked on several beach party films like *Beach Blanket Bingo* and *How to Stuff a Wild Bikini* costarring with Annette Funicello and Frankie Avalon.

His final film appearance was in the 1966 motion picture *A Funny Thing Happened on the Way to the Forum,* costarring Phil Silvers and Zero Mostel. This film featured an all-star cast of comedy giants, giving Keaton a sense of relief to perform with old friends. Jack Gilford, Alfie Bass, and John Bluthal rounding out the cast of comedy greats.

As with several of his contemporaries, Keaton had great success on the screen but seemed to suffer in the reality of everyday life. Keaton met and married actress Natalie Talmadge, daughter of the founder of Talmadge studios and known with her sisters as "The Talmadge Sisters." The two married and had two sons together. After the birth of their second son, Talmadge turned Keaton away and eventually divorced him, taking his entire fortune and the two boys with her in the divorce. After the divorce, Keaton was forced to declare bankruptcy and was sued by the Internal Revenue Service for twenty-eight thousand dollars in back taxes. He suffered at the hands of his estranged wife and the government, turning to alcohol for comfort. This landed Keaton in an institution for a period of time to sober up and work through his personal issues. During this time, he married one of the nurses in what he claims was an alcoholic blackout. The marriage only last one year, and, once again, his wife claimed most of what was left of his fortune in the divorce.

Keaton remained single until 1940, when he met Eleanor Morris, who was twenty-three years his junior. Morris devoted herself to helping Keaton become sober and revive his waning career. The two were married until Keaton died in 1966.

Keaton worked right up until his death. The comedian had been diagnosed with advanced lung cancer but was not told of his condition's severity until the final months of his life. He performed many of his own stunts on the set of his final picture, although the studio heads were concerned about his health with the exertion on screen.

Buster Keaton died of lung cancer on February 1, 1966, in Woodland Hills, California. The Guardian newspaper offered a tribute to the comedian on February 2, 1966:

Buster Keaton, who died yesterday in Hollywood, was something of a genius, and even today there are men who spend hours arguing whether Charlie Chaplin or Harry Langdon or Buster Keaton *was the greatest of the comedians of Hollywood's vintage years, when custard pies were delivered in every reel.*

No one will ever provide the answer to suit everyone. But Keaton, who would have been 70 this year, is enshrined in the memories of all who saw him as one of the three great comedians who made silent pictures an art. Unlike his rivals, he continued to act until almost the end of his life; he retired only four months ago when the lung cancer, which killed him, made work – even in television commercials – impossible...

The funeral for Keaton was held at Forest Lawn Memorial Park in the Hollywood Hills, with Dick Van Dyke giving the eulogy at the service.

Keaton was buried at Forest Lawn Memorial Park, just steps away from comedy great Stan Laurel.

Roscoe "Fatty" Arbuckle

Roscoe Arbuckle was born in Smith Center, Kansas, on March 24, 1887, one of nine children to Mary Gordon and William Arbuckle. The family moved to Santa Ana, California, when Arbuckle was two years old, and Roscoe began performing at the age of eight at a local theater.

By the time he was ten, Arbuckle was entering amateur shows and began performing in carnivals, traveling stock companies, and eventually on the Vaudeville circuit. A large child, he amazed audiences with his agility at physical comedy, performing acrobatics, magic, and songs on stage. Arbuckle's mother passed away when he was just eleven years old, and this forced Arbuckle to support himself when his father refused to support him. Arbuckle took jobs in local hotels to earn a living. Arbuckle was discovered singing on the job, and he was invited to sing in a local amateur contest. During this performance, Arbuckle delighted audiences with his physical comedy, which won him the first prize.

Arbuckle attempted to get into the burgeoning film industry several times before studio head Mack Sennett hired Arbuckle at Keystone Studios in 1913. Arbuckle became an instant success playing opposite great comedic actors like Mabel Normand and Charlie Chaplin. Within a year, Arbuckle was writing all of his own material and directing most of the films he starred in.

By 1917, Arbuckle had taken over creative control of the Comique Film Corporation under producer Joseph Schenck's direction. During this time, Arbuckle met and nurtured a young Buster Keaton, whom he considered a comedic genius. Within a short time, Arbuckle allowed Keaton to write most of his gags and direct the films he was starring in.

From 1917 through 1921, Arbuckle enjoyed continuous success, producing two-reel comedies and eventually moving up to full-length feature films. Some of his best-known films include *Butcher Boy* in 1917, *Out West* in 1918, and *Back Stage* in 1919. In 1921 Arbuckle received an enormous salary increase and decided to take a trip to San Francisco for labor day weekend with friends for some well-deserved rest.

Arbuckle and his company arrived at the St. Francis hotel and stayed in adjoining suites 1219, 1220, and 1221. The celebration lasted for several days, but on September 5, a young starlet, Virginia Rappe, became suddenly ill and was rushed to a local hospital. She died four days later of peritonitis due to a ruptured bladder. Several of the guests accused Arbuckle of raping and killing the young girl even though none of them witnessed what they accused Arbuckle of perpetrating. Several San Francisco newspapers ran headlines with graphic details of events that were pure fiction. Arbuckle was arrested and put on trial for the murder of Rappe and suffered every indignation during the trial. At the end of the drama, Arbuckle was tried three different times, the first two juries unable to come to a unanimous decision causing two mistrials.

Finally, in 1922, Arbuckle was tried for the third time, and the jury found him innocent on all counts and offering the following verdict:

"Acquittal is not enough for Roscoe Arbuckle. We feel that a great injustice has been done him. We feel also that it was our only plain duty to give him this exoneration. There was not the slightest proof adduced to connect him in any way with the commission of a crime."

Even though Arbuckle was absolved of the crime, this was not good enough for the Hollywood studios or audiences. With the scandal of Arbuckle and several other indiscretions by some of Hollywood's top stars, the studio's hired Will H. Hays to head a self-policing organization called the Hays Code for Censorship of American Film to clean up Hollywood and get rid of the undesirable elements.

On April 18, 1922, Arbuckle was banned from the film industry, ending a once-unstoppable career. The ban was lifted months later, in December 1922, but the damage to Arbuckle's career had been done by then. Arbuckle could not find work anywhere in Hollywood. Years later, Arbuckle began directing films under a pseudonym, William Goodrich, and co-owned a popular nightclub.

In 1932, some of Arbuckle's contemporaries began a letter-writing campaign to the studios asking for Arbuckle's come back. He began once again making two-reel comedies to modest success. Finally, Arbuckle began receiving the acclaim he once enjoyed at the onset of his career.

Warner Brother approached him with a lucrative contract, and Arbuckle agreed. On the evening of June 28, 1933, Arbuckle went to dinner with his wife to celebrate their wedding anniversary after signing the contract. When the couple returned to their home, Arbuckle went to bed and suffered a massive heart attack killing him where he lay. His body was discovered in the early hours of June 29, 1933, by his wife of one year, Addie Oakley Dukes McPhail.

The funeral for Arbuckle was held at the Frank E. Campbell funeral home in New York City. Arbuckle was dressed in a dark grey suit with his ever-present bowtie in place. The gray steel casket with silver handles was placed in the gold room, the same visitation room that held Rudolph Valentino's body seven years earlier. Over twelve thousand fans filed past the great man who fell from grace. Good friend Buster Keaton attended the funeral, as well as Bert Lahr and Ray McCarey. Will Rogers gave a touchingly tearful eulogy for his friend.

After the service, Arbuckle was cremated, and his remains scattered in the pacific ocean.

Ben Turpin

Ben Turpin, the cross-eyed comedian of stage, screen, and circus' whose mega-stardom rivaled that of Charlie Chaplin and Buster Keaton's. While he was one of the highest-paid and best-known actors of his time, Turpin's memory and acclaim have faded into obscurity over the generations. Only those fans of the great silent era of film that have kept the memory of this dazzling film star alive.

The statistical information about Ben Turpin is shady at best, his birth date is recorded as September 17th, but the year of his birth varies anywhere from 1869 to 1874. Bernard Turpin was born in New Orleans, Louisiana, to a candy store owner. The family moved regularly throughout the United States, his father attempting to find success with different businesses in different locations.

The story of how Turpin's eyes became crossed is another story without confirmation. It is unknown whether he was born with the affliction or the abnormality came from a childhood mishap. Turpin told so many different versions of the incident throughout his life that there is no true record of the events.

It is rumored that in his teen years, Turpin was given one hundred dollars by his father to make a start in the world and Turpin squandered the money rather than investing it in a business or his future. The story continues that Turpin ran away from home and jumped on a tramp steamer rather than face his father's wrath after squandering the money. The next years of his life are hazy as Turpin never told the same account of these early years twice. He claimed to have been a bum, traveling from town to town, perfecting his physical comedy, and learning how to take a fall without breaking any bones. He stated in interviews that he performed in the circus and in Vaudeville throughout the U.S., finally settling in Chicago.

Whether these stories are true or not has been lost to history, but his life changed dramatically for the better in 1907.

That year, Turpin took a job with Essanay studios as a janitor and part-time actor. The studio used Turpin as a bit player, never capitalizing on Turpin's unusual facial features or vigorous physical pratfalls. In 1909, Turpin appeared in the motion picture *Mr. Flip* directed by Gilbert "Broncho Billy" Anderson. It was in this film that Turpin received his first pie in the face, a classic funny bit that would become a comedy staple in silent films.

Turpin began to make a name for himself with Essanay studios, but in 1915, Charlie Chaplin signed a contract with Essanay, making Turpin a supporting player once again. It is said that Turpin did not enjoy working with Chaplin since the two men had dramatically different styles of acting comedy and Chaplin getting the lion's share of attention from producers and directors. Chaplin worked on the subtleties of the film, while Turpin was much more straightforward in his interpretations of the script. Chaplin did not last long with Essanay Studios, and the film company was soon finding it difficult to compete with the west coast studios. Turpin stayed on with Essanay until 1917 when he signed with Mack Sennett and Keystone Studios. Turpin was cast in dozens of films for Sennett, always playing in character roles for maximum effect. He enjoyed great success spoofing the more popular films and actors of the 1920s like Rudolph Valentino.

Turpin's eyes were his trademark, and he was always concerned about the deformity correcting itself and losing his livelihood. Turpin took out an insurance policy with Lloyd's of London® just in case, easing his mind. Another rumor surfaced that Turpin, being a devote Catholic, was teased by his contemporaries claiming they would pray for his eyes to be uncrossed so others could enjoy success in the movies as well. Turpin became one of the highest-paid actors during his time with Sennett, making three thousand dollars a week, a feat he was quite proud of.

In 1929, with the advent of the talking pictures, Turpin decided to retire to care for his ailing wife rather than reinventing himself into the talkies. He invested his money in real estate and retired to a comfortable life where he never needed to work again.

The studios continued to clamor for Turpin's unique comedy style, offering him roles in several pictures. Turpin demanded a flat one-thousand-dollar fee for each appearance, whether it was a bit part or starring role. He appeared in only a handful of films over the next ten years. The 1929 film *The Love Parade*, *Keystone Hotel* in 1935 and, his final film, *Saps at Sea* in 1940, starring opposite Laurel and Hardy.

Turpin lived quite comfortably in his golden years, working part-time as a plumber in one of his many apartment houses in Los Angeles. On July 1, 1940, Turpin suffered a fatal heart attack that ended his life.

The funeral for Ben Turpin was held at Forest Lawn Memorial Park in Glendale, California. The star was buried in the Great Mausoleum in a private family room within the immense mausoleum. His crypt marked by a bronze plate with his signature scrolled across the crypt front.

W.C. Fields

An American icon of comedy, W.C. Fields was loved by audiences for his contemptuous look at the world with unwavering hatred for women, children, and animals alike.

William Claude Dukenfield was born the first of five children to an English family that immigrated to American in the year 1854. The family lived in Darby, Pennsylvania; when Fields was born, his father worked as a hotel clerk and produce merchant to feed his family.

Fields began performing at the age of fifteen, learning to be a master juggler. The family encouraged Fields to perform, allowing the boy to perform for churches and local theaters while attending school.

Fields entered Vaudeville, honing his comedy style and continuing to thrill audiences with his juggling act.

During this time, Fields made a name for himself as W.C. Fields "The Eccentric Juggler," his new moniker becoming a headliner in Europe and North America. Within a few years, Fields was known as an international celebrity, juggling everything from balls to cigar boxes, using pantomime as a universal way to communicate with his audiences worldwide.

In 1900, Fields met and married fellow Vaudevillian Harriet Hughes. The two were married on April 8, 1900, and four years later, they had a son, William Claude Fields. Hughes desperately wanted Fields to settle down to normal family life, but Fields refused to give up on touring in the U.S. and Europe. While Fields was performing in England, Hattie separated from her husband, unable to withstand the separations for such long periods. Fields continued to stay in contact with Hughes and sent monthly child support payments without reservation. While the couple was separated from 1904, they stayed legally married until his death in 1946.

Fields became a parent once again in 1917, fathering another son with girlfriend Bessie Poole. Sadly, Poole was killed only a few years later in a bar fight, and the son was left in foster care. Fields voluntarily supported the child, sending payments to the foster family each month to ensure the child's welfare.

In 1915, Fields made his first attempt at breaking into cinema. He appeared in only a couple of films, his theater commitments keeping him extremely busy. Finally, in 1924, Fields appeared in the film *Sally of the Sawdust*, his first feature role. Fields appeared regularly in silent films until 1932 when he signed a contract with

Paramount Pictures and began making feature-length films. Within two years, Fields was a major movie star and writing his own ticket in Hollywood. Between 1933 and 1935, Fields performed in some of his best work with films like *Tillie and Gus*, *You're Telling Me*, *Mississippi,* and in his masterpieces of the era, *The Old-Fashioned Way. It's a Gift,* and *The Man on the Flying Trapeze* followed quickly after continuing Fields' great success. In 1935, Fields was offered the role of Mr. Micawber in the film *David Copperfield* directed by Frank Cukor. Fields was honored at the request and asked Paramount if he could work for MGM studios while under contract with them. Paramount agreed, and Fields went on to make the classic film that would become a classic in cinema.

Fields, a master of improvisation, was known to change any script he was given to suit his talents. While Fields maintained the basic theme of any scene he was performing, little of the original dialogue was known to remain in the scene.

The parts Fields played in many of the films he starred in were generally swindlers, con men, or gambling sharks. Fields loved playing the cranky old man who hated children and animals or the hen-pecked husband with the domineering wife. Some chose to believe the cantankerous con artist was Fields' true persona, but it is generally known that Fields had a great fondness for children.

In 1939, Fields was the second choice to play the wizard in the classic film *The Wizard of Oz*. He chose not to take the role, as Fields had a prior commitment to do the film *You Can't Cheat an Honest Man*. Some say that

45

fields turned down the role because of financial reasons, but this was never substantiated.

Some of Fields' trademarks were his bulbous red nose and propensity for drinking. While Fields was a known alcoholic in his later years, he did not touch a drop of alcohol until the age of thirty-five. Being a stage performer and juggler, Fields was required to maintain his concentration, which could not be accomplished without being sober.

Once fields began acting, he was known to have a bottle with him at all times. Even with his love of drinking, Fields maintained his ever-present professionalism, having no complaints of poor behavior on the set until 1936, when the drinking consumed his life. Fields was known to put away up to two quarts of gin per day, causing him to have periods of delirium tremens, which caused severe shaking, rapid heart rate, fever, and perspiration. Paramount finally released Fields from his contract leaving the actor to find a new vocation for his talents.

Fields began appearing on *The Chase and Sanborn Hour* radio show starring Edgar Bergen and puppet Charlie McCarthy. The banter between Fields and McCarthy made for classic radio comedy, and Fields maintained his star status while taking the time to improve his health. However, he continued drinking during his recovery.

In 1939, Fields began working with Universal Studios on a four-film contract, teaming him up with Bergen and McCarthy for *You Can't Cheat an Honest Man*. Fields turned down the role of the wizard in The Wizard of Oz to work on this film. He also starred in the 1940 film, *My Little Chickadee,* opposite the voluptuous

Mae West. It is rumored that Fields walked off the set after what some described as a minor disagreement with director Edward Cline. The director was required to use a body double to finish the film when Fields did not return to finish shooting.

Fields' final starring role came with the picture *Never Give a Sucker an Even Break* in 1941, costarring Gloria Jean and Leon Errol. Fields hoped Universal Studios would offer him a full-time contract after the final film wrapped, but the offer never materialized. Fields never work in a leading role again and worked less frequently as the decade progressed.

By 1946, Fields' health was failing, and cirrhosis of the liver caused his abdomen to swell. Fields sold all of his possessions and moved into Los Encinas Sanitarium in Los Angeles, California, where he rented a private bungalow. Fields told tales of how he spent his last days reading the bible, looking for loopholes.

W.C. Fields died on Christmas day of 1946 at the age of sixty-six. The New York Times obituary gave a tribute to the comedian on December 26, 1946:

W.C. Fields, 66, Dies; Famed as Comedian
By BOSLEY CROWTHER

Pasadena, Calif., Dec. 25--W. C. Fields, the comedian whose deadpan gestures, raspy remarks and "never give a sucker an even break" characterizations made him a showman beloved the nation over, died today at the age of 66.

He was equally well know in show business for his ad libbing and complete disregard for prepared scripts, either in the movies or radio. Once he said that the only lines he followed truly were those of Charles Dickens.

Fields got his first job in show business as a juggler at a summer part in Norristown, Pa., at $5 a week.

Left Home at Age of 11

Few men have contributed as much to the world's merriment as W. C. Fields. The comedian who ran away from home when he was 11 years old, who starved and suffered and was forced to live on his wits, kept his sense of the ridiculous-- developing it, indeed, it would seem, with every hard knock he received in his youth.

His capital consisted of a highly expressive face, with a bulbous nose as the main feature, a fine voice for comedy purposes and a profound capacity for punishment. Of earthly goods he had little until he blossomed forth as one of the really great comedians about the year 1924.

His art has been described erroneously as that of the slapstick and clownerie. It is true that he could out-slapstick and out-clown most funny men of stage, circus or screen, but he possessed just a little more than his contemporaries. He was a master mimic, inimitable in his droll asides, an improviser and innovator of new tricks.

Some years ago when a whole cast of screen stars were picked to take parts in "Alice in Wonderland" he easily outshone the others in his conception of Humpty Dumpty. The voice alone carried him to one of his greatest artistic triumphs in that egg disguise.

He is remembered for his notable presentation of Micawber in "David Copperfield." Other successes of the screen in which he played major parts include "The Great McGonigle," "Tillie and Gus," "Six of a Kind," "Mrs. Wiggs of the Cabbage Patch," "Mississippi" and "The Man on the Flying Trapeze."

During the last ten years the principal Fields films were "Poppy," "The Big Broadcast of 1938," "You Can't Cheat an Honest Man," "My Little Chickadee," written by Mae West and Mr. Fields and starring both; "The Bank Dick" and "Never Give a Sucker an Even Break."

It was rumored that Fields had three funeral services. One non-denominational service where Edgar Bergen gave the eulogy. According to Bergen, Fields stated to him before he died, "If I ever found a church that didn't believe in knocking all the other churches, I might consider joining it."

Fields was cremated, and his remains were placed in a niche inside the Great Mausoleum at Forest Lawn Memorial Park in Glendale, California. A simple bronze plate adorns the niche with his name, year of birth, and year of death only.

Mabel Normand

One of the first women of the silent era to not only act but write, direct, and produce, Mabel Normand was considered a versatile actress and comedienne during her brief period in Hollywood history. The evolution of silent films could not be adequately conveyed without including this pivotal woman and her contribution to silent comedy. Known as one of the first "Movie Stars," Normand began her career at the onset of motion picture films, capitalizing on the international media. However, this media attention worked against her at the height of her career.

Mabel Normand was born Mabel Ethelreid Normand on November 10, 1895 in Staten Island, New York. The youngest of three children, her father worked as a carpenter in local theaters, also playing the piano for the live acts that came into the theater to entertain audiences. His meager income leaving her family to live at the poverty level for most of Normand's childhood. Normand enjoyed music and art during her school years. During an interview, she recalled practicing at the piano for seven or eight hours a day whenever she got the chance. While her musical talents were never fully realized, she never lost her passion for music until her death. Normand began working as a model at the age of sixteen and began taking bit parts in the new flickers in 1910. She starred in her first motion picture that same year, *Indiscretions of Betty,* a short about a woman living far beyond her husband's income.

Normand went to work for D.W. Griffith for American Mutoscope Biography pictures in New York doing short subject films and two-reel comedies in 1911. Griffith had no desire to use Normand consistently and when the company moved west to Central California, Normand stayed behind seeking work with Vitagraph pictures performing opposite actors like John Bunny and Max Linder. It was during this time Normand learned all she could about acting in front of the camera. The understated gesture or the facial expression that could convey feelings without overacting or pantomiming served Normand for the rest of her career.

Normand was adaptable to dramatic roles as well as comedy during this time and showed her excellence in both mediums. The company moved to Southern California, as most of the studios were migrating West due to the agreeable weather in Southern California. Normand was reassigned to the comedy unit headed by Mack Sennett. The two started a love affair that might explain why Normand appeared as the star of so many early comedies. Many believe that Normand's ability to create dangerous situations and harrowing thrills kept Sennett from using the actress in the feature films.

In 1912, Sennett convinced Normand to leave her steady work with Vitagraph and brought her to work for him when Sennett founded Keystone Studios.

Normand had a flare for comedy that made her a huge box office draw and was starred in many of Sennett's two-reel comedies playing opposite the greats like Charlie Chaplin and Roscoe Arbuckle. It is rumored that when Chaplin came to Keystone, Sennett, at first, regretted his decision but was asked by Normand to give Chaplin a chance. Sennett finally assigned Normand as the director of Chaplin's next film *Mabel at the Wheel,* in which the two starred opposite each other. Chaplin regarded this as a slap in the face to his abilities, and tempers flared on the set with Chaplin pushing back at Normand's directing style. Sennett finally stepped in and met with Chaplin in his dressing room; allegedly, the meeting ended with Sennett leaving, slamming the dressing room door in a fit of rage. They completed the filming, but Sennett had to concede to Chaplin's demands and allow the man to direct himself because of the popularity he was creating with his pictures. In time, Normand and Chaplin resigned to work together, appearing in several popular comedies.

It is rumored that, in 1915, Mabel walked in on Sennett with his mistress in the throes of passion, and the woman hurtled a vase at Normand's head, which causes severe injury. While it is true that Normand suffered a serious injury at this time, there is no evidence of the gossip being true. Normand was in the hospital and convalesced for several weeks, and the romance between her and Sennett ended abruptly; the two never fully trusted each other again. Not too long after this injury, Normand found herself once again injured on the set, which was the start of serious health problems that would plague her for the rest of her life.

Normand played every genre of heroine on the screen, from school teachers to damsels in distress, tomboys to debutants. In 1917, Normand signed with the newly formed Goldwyn film studio and began working for Goldwyn. The working relationship quickly became an affair between the head of the studio and Normand, and it was rumored that Normand suffered a miscarriage as a result of the affair. Once again, there are no records to confirm this, and all that remains are stories. Normand also reportedly began a party lifestyle, turning up late on the set, which caused problems for the actress with the studio. Several costars and studio people spoke of her hard-drinking and late nights, which showed up on the screen with lackluster performances and her appearance taking a dramatic turn.

February 1, 1922, Normand found herself in the middle of a scandal involving director William Desmond Taylor. Normand arrived at Taylor's home and stayed one hour, purportedly discussing some new books Taylor had just purchase. Taylor walked Normand to her car and waved as the actress drove away. The next morning Normand received the call that Taylor had been murdered sometime after Normand was seen leaving the residence. While Normand was never charged with the murder, police investigated her, and many of her private letters were made public, causing the actress to lose favor with her fans. The media distorted facts, making it seem that Normand had much more to do with the death than was ever proven. Police and reporters hounded Normand to the point that she traveled to Europe in 1922 just to keep her sanity.

Even with the public embarrassment, Normand's next film, *Susanna,* was a modest success, and Sennett cast Normand in *The Extra Girl* the next year. She continued working steadily with audiences forgiving her for her involvement with the scandal. Unfortunately for Normand, scandal would find her again at a dinner party in November 1923 when She arrived at Edna Purviance's home. Edna's beau Courtland S. Dines insulted Normand during the dinner, and she left early; stepping into her limousine, she shared the distasteful ordeal with her chauffeur. He took her home then returned to Purviance's home to confront Dines. When Dines refused, Greer pulled out a revolver and shot Dines, which killed him. While Normand was completely exonerated for the crime, her career suffered greatly; her films were banned in the U.S. Normand refused to take this lying down and, in April 1924, she went on the tour of the country to promote her next film, *The Extra Girl.* The publicity stunt worked, and Normand's films were once again welcomed into the theaters.

In 1926, Normand signed with Hal Roach studios and continued working even though she was slowing down. That same year, Normand married longtime actor Lew Cody; the two having known each other from previous work. It was rumored that Cody had asked Normand to marry him many times but, at a dinner party with friends, he proposed, and she said yes. Cody then dared Normand to marry him, and the two were husband and wife by the next morning.

February 15, 1927, Normand was admitted into the hospital with a headline in the New York Times claiming the actress was suffering from pneumonia. Normand's health had begun to decline rapidly, and she was diagnosed with tuberculosis in December of 1928. Normand was admitted to a sanitarium in September 1929, where she continued battling the disease until her death on February 23, 1930. She succumbed to the disease at the age of thirty-seven.

The funeral of Mabel Normand was held on March 3, 1930. Among the pallbearers were Louis B. Mayer, Judge James, Eugene Pallette, Charlie Chaplin, and Sid Grauman. Fellow notables at the service included Douglas Fairbanks Sr., Colonel Art Goebel, D.W. Griffith, Mack Sennett, and Samuel Goldwyn.

Mabel Normand was laid to rest at Calvary Cemetery in Los Angeles, California. Her white marble crypt displays the name "Mabel Normand Cody" with her birth and death years. A simple epitaph reads, "Rest in Peace."

Mack Sennett

Known as the king of the comedies, Mack Sennett is best remembered for his innovations to the art of filmmaking at the advent of silent movies. Sennett's creation of the slapstick comedy made him a force in the motion picture, both on the east coast and Hollywood, dominating the motion picture comedy industry.

Mack Sennett was born in Danville, Quebec, Canada; his given name Mikall Sinnott. Sennett and his family moved to Northampton, Massachusetts, when he was seventeen, where Sennett finished his education in the United States. At this time, Sennett went to his first Vaudeville show and was intrigued by what he saw on the stage. Sennet watched the various performers on the stage as they show off their talents in singing, dancing, and comedy while the audience laughed and clapped for their favorites. Instantly, Sennett desired to become a performer himself but to the disappointment of his mother.

In 1902, Sennett moved to New York with the help of a friend, Marie Dressler, where he refined his talents as an actor, singer, and dancer. He worked backstage in the theaters where he began set designing and, finally, was hired as an actor in the fledgling field of motion pictures with Biograph Studios in 1908. Sennett starred with some of the top names that paved the way for the new motion pictures. Mary Pickford and Mabel Normand became good friends with Sennett, and the trio appeared together in the short subjects numerous times. By 1910, Sennett began directing films enjoying working behind the camera as much as acting. Sennett worked day and night to learn all of the techniques of motion picture technology, his directing style taken from his years working in the theater.

By 1912, Sennett decided he was ready for total creative control of his movies. Adam Kessel and Charles O. Bauman of the New York Motion Picture Company put up the money for Sennett to create Keystone Studios. He moved out west to Edendale, California, where the weather was perfect for filming all year-round.

Sennett was now able to make the kind of motion pictures he envisioned. Wild car chases and custard pie throwing antics were only some of the comedy devices Sennett used to keep the audiences in stitches. Mabel Normand, W.C. Fields, Charlie Chaplin, and Ford Sterling were just a few of the actors made famous by their association with Sennett. His films not only had the gift of comedy but a bevy of beautiful girls who became known as the "Sennett Bathing Beauties" featured in the films for the benefit of the male audience.

Sennett, in 1917, decided to create a new film corporation, Mack Sennett Comedies Corporation. While the Keystone name continued, the film's quality became poor and, eventually, dropped out of favor with audiences. On the other hand, Sennett began making feature-length films, and his star continued to rise in Hollywood.

In 1920, Sennett began making some poor choices with the films he was distributing to the public. He partnered with Pathe Films and circulated their two-reel films at an alarming rate. This, coupled with other studios jumping on the bandwagon to distributed their films at the same rate, flooded the market, causing Sennett to lose market share. Sennett refused to cut costs or change his methods even when his films were no longer profitable.

Sennett, always the innovator, saw the invention of talking films in the late 1920s as a new opportunity, rather than a flash in the pan as most of the other studios predicted. Sennett began making talking subject films and released them through Educational Pictures. In 1932, Sennett was nominated for an Academy Award® for *The Loud Mouth*, a live-action short film. Sennett worked with the top stars of the day; his relationship with Bing Crosby was instrumental in getting him a partnership with Paramount Pictures.

While this partnership only last one year, the distribution deal was another bad business dealing for Sennett. The final blow financially came after Sennett lost everything in the stock market crash of 1929. By November 1933, Sennett was forced to declare bankruptcy.

His last work as Producer/Director came in 1935 with *The Timid Young Man* starring Buster Keaton and *Way Up Thar* starring Joan Davis. Sennett retired at the age of 55 with over one thousand silent pictures and dozens of talking pictures produced during his twenty-five years in the film industry. Sennett was awarded an honorary Academy Award® in 1938 for his contributions to film.

While Sennett enjoyed his retirement, he infrequently appeared on television and made a few cameo appearances in popular shows.

Sennett died on November 6, 1960, at the age of eighty. Family and friends attended his funeral, and Sennett was laid to rest at Holy Cross Cemetery in Culver City, California. A simple granite headstone adorns the grave with the epitaph, "Beloved King of Comedy."

Eddie Cantor

Eddie Cantor was loved by audiences nationwide with his hilarious comedic antics, the eye-rolling song and dance man of the stage, screen, and television. Cantor was best known for his Nicknamed "Banjo Eyes," created after a caricature was drawn of him with huge, circular eyes in the shape of the banjo by artist Frederick J. Garner.

Raised by his grandmother and living in New York, Eddie Cantor began his career with appearances in local talent contests. Encouraged by his grandmother, Cantor performed regularly in local theaters. By the time he was in his late teens, Cantor had worked as a waiter/performer at a Coney Island saloon with a young piano player named Jimmy Durante accompanying him.

Cantor changed his name from his given name Isadore or Izzy, as his friends and family liked to call him, to Eddie in 1903. When it was suggested that Izzy was not a good comedy name by his future wife, Ida Tobias, Eddie took the advice and began to bill himself as Eddie Cantor

Cantor began working in Vaudeville in 1907 at New York's Clinton Music Hall. Cantor toured steadily for the next few years and met fellow comedian Lila Lee during his time on the road. The two comedians decided to create an act together and toured as Cantor & Lee. The duo caught the attention of renowned theater producer Florenz Ziegfield famous for his Ziegfeld Follies.

Cantor was offered a part in the production of the stage show *Midnight Frolic,* and Cantor jumped at the chance to be involved in the production. His beloved grandmother passed away just two days before he signed the contract with Ziegfield. Cantor worked with the Zigfield Follies for the next ten years as a song and dance man, to critical and box office acclaim. Cantor also began composing during his time with The Follies, writing several popular tunes like *Every Blossom I See Reminds Me of You* and *I Found a Baby on My Door Step.*

After his time on Broadway, Cantor appeared on *Rudy Vallee's The Fleischmann's Yeast Hour and The Chase and Sanborn Hour* radio programs. Cantor became an enormous star on the radio, charming audiences with his songs and comedy. Cantor was instrumental in introducing singer Dinah Shore to his audience featuring the young woman on his radio show.

In 1934, Cantor was asked to introduce a new song on his show. The song had been turned down by most of the popular shows of the day, but Cantor found the song charming, and *Santa Claus is Coming to Town* hit the airwaves. Over one hundred thousand copies of the sheet music were ordered the next day, making the tune a hit song of that year.

Throughout the 1940s and early 1950s, Cantor maintained a top spot on the radio, drawing in crowds of listeners to his *Time to Smile* show.

While Cantor enjoyed enormous success, he made some career choices he regretted along the way. In 1929, he was offered the starring role in a new talking picture, *The Jazz Singer*. The part had been turned down by actor George Jessel, and Cantor decided the role would not be a good vehicle for his career; the part eventually went to Al Jolson, making Jolson a movie star.

Politically, Cantor was very outspoken, participating in the 1919 strike to form Actor Equity along with one hundred and nineteen other stage actors. This angered Ziegfeld, almost causing him to lose his part in The Follies. In 1939, Cantor once again used his fame as a platform to denounce Father Charles Coughlin for the priest's use of radio to denounce the Jewish culture using anti-Semitic commentary. Sponsor Camel cigarettes canceled sponsorship of his show as a result of his outspokenness.

Although the stock market crash of 1929 wiped out Cantor and many others' fortune, Cantor used his talents to continue songwriting and publish bestselling cartoon books. He soon found himself with plenty of funds while others struggled for years to regain even a small part of their fortunes.

Cantor also capitalized on films during the 1940s, appearing in several feature films like *Whoopee!, Ali Baba Goes to Town,* and *If you Knew Susie.*

In the 1950s, with the beginnings of television, Cantor hosted *The Colgate Comedy Hour* variety show. The show was wildly popular with audiences but was canceled abruptly when a young Sammy Davis Jr. appeared as a guest, and Cantor mopped Davis's brow after his performance. This upset the sponsors, who told Cantor they would cancel the show if he had Davis on again. Cantor's response to the threats was to book Davis for two solid weeks.

During his radio days, Cantor was instrumental in the charity to combat childhood polio and coined the term "The March of Dimes," a nonprofit organization to benefit the health of mothers and their children. Cantor asked audiences to mail one dime to then-President Franklin Delano Roosevelt. This act of charity caught on, and soon other celebrities began asking the public for their contributions. Cantor also entertained the troops during World War II tirelessly, traveling throughout Europe to bring laughter to troops fighting for freedom. It is generally unknown, but Cantor used this opportunity to assist men, women, and children to safety from war zones by boat.

In 1952, Cantor suffered the first of two heart attacks causing him to semi-retire from show business. Cantor enjoyed his golden years, continuing his writing and the occasional television appearance. Cantor suffered a personal loss with the death of his daughter Margie in 1959 and his wife Ida in 1962.

In 1964, Cantor was given an honorary Academy Award® for his contribution to the art of film.

Eddie Cantor died of a fatal heart attack on October 10, 1964, at the age of seventy-two.

The New York Times obituary ran on October 11, 1964:

HOLLYWOOD, Oct. 10—Eddie Cantor, banjo-eyed vaudevillian whose dancing feet and double-takes brought him stardom in movies, radio and television, died of a coronary occlusion today at the age of 72.

The comedian, famed for his charitable works, continued to be a show-business figure a decade after giving up public appearances.

Semi-retired since suffering a heart seizure in 1953, Mr. Cantor wrote books and took pride in his discovery of new talent. His energy and drive, which led to the severe heart condition, made him one of the best-loved performers of his generation.

Ida Cantor, his wife, died Aug. 8, 1962, at the age of 70. She became Known to millions of Americans because of her husband's theme song, "Ida," and the jokes he used to tell about his family. Mrs. Cantor died of a series of heart seizures.

Cantor was interred in the mausoleum at Hillside Memorial Park in Culver City, California. A simple bronze plate with the epitaph reading "Husband, Father, and Grandfather.

John Bunny

Known as "the man who makes more than the president," John Bunny was the first comedy star of the silent film era. Bunny paved the way for the comedic actors that followed him to create a world where laughter could be used as a universal language. Little did he know that within a short time of his death, Bunny would be all but forgotten in a world where he was a leader during his lifetime.

John Bunny was born to a family of English sea captains in 1863 in Brooklyn, New York. His family assumed that Bunny would fall in line with tradition to become yet another man of the ocean; regrettably, this was not something they would see happen for the family.

While attending school at St. James high school in New York City, Bunny learned to box, swim, and a variety of sports at which he excelled. While little is known about his early years, Bunny lived a simple life with his family while attending school.

Bunny discovered a love for the theater as a young man. He worked as a grocery clerk but could not disregard the still small voice inside that longed for a career on the stage. He ran away from home and joined a traveling mistral show in the late 1800s. Traveling and performing, Bunny learned his craft from the likes of Lew Fields and Hattie Williams, some of the top actors on the Vaudeville circuit.

Having heard about the new invention known as "The Flickers," Bunny left the stage show and went to work for Vitagraph studio. For Bunny, this was a step down in status and in pay going from making one hundred and fifty dollars a week to forty dollars a week.

Over the next five years, Bunny made over one hundred and fifty short films with Vitagraph and became a worldwide celebrity. Bunny was not considered an attractive leading man type for the cinema, but rather a comic player with his short stature and three-hundred-pound frame. Bunny stated in an interview:

" I didn't aim to be a comedian, but nature was agin' me. How could I hope to play Romeo with a figure like mine? It was many years before I learned to yield gracefully to the fate for which nature endowed me."

His gnome-like face was his distinguishing feature and commented on by report John Palmer for the Saturday Review:

"Mr. Bunny has an extensive and extremely flexible face. When he smells a piece of gorgonzola cheese there is no doubt whatever that his nose has been seriously offended. When he sees for the first time a pretty and eligible young woman, there is no doubt whatever that he is immensely excited and moved with intentions so extravagantly honorable that they seem almost too grievous to be borne. Mr. Bunny's emotions are all on the grand scale. His despair is incredible. His grief is unendurable. His smile is an ignis fatuus."

In his first film for Vitagraph, Bunny was paid only five dollars and played the father of a girl about to get married. After this first attempt on screen, the studio offered Bunny forty dollars a week to become a contract player. While this was a fraction of the amount Bunny had made on the legitimate stage, he accepted the terms and went to work for Vitagraph Studios. Bunny was used anywhere he was needed in a film, sometimes playing a lead role or at other times playing bit parts. In time, Bunny became one of the driving forces for Vitagraph and was offered a series of short films playing the lead role.

Co-starring with Bunny was actress Flora Finch. The duo had done several films together before the studio decided to pair them for a series of films. The motion pictures they made together were known as "Bunnygraphs" or "Bunnyfinches." Finch's tall, lean frame was in stark contrast to Bunny's stature, and this made for a successful partnership. Bunny playing the everyday man who would get satisfaction from sneaking behind his wife's back to play pool, gamble at the race track or play poker with the boys. While the duo portrayed amazing chemistry on set, the studio head, Albert E. Smith, claimed the pair hated each other profusely; he claimed that Bunny was arrogant, bad-tempered, and difficult to work with.

Larry Trimble's daughter also states in the book *The Big V,* "He was very bad-tempered, very difficult. He upstaged everyone. He was an old egocentric. He always wanted the camera on him. He wasn't as mean as W.C. Fields, but he was verging on it."

Apart from Bunny's successful movies during his five years in the film industry, Bunny is also known as the first movie star to die at the top of his popularity. In one interview made just one month before his death, Bunny made statements that could be considered an eerie prophecy of what was to come:

> "I shall live longer than Irving and Booth, not because I deserve to, but because there is a record of me that they did not leave; the public can have me always the same, so long as the pictures are preserved. To be remembered the feet must move. It is the single photograph that gets put away, but throw me on the screen when I am only ashes and the people will respond the way they always responded. Indeed, I would wager that they would rise up and become enthusiastic toward a dead comedy actor who, in pictures, went right on amusing them with over country rides in pursuit of a runaway daughter. It has a tang of the game in it. Most dead people are dead for a long while, but the moving picture actor goes right on living and loving and laughing and walking, even if he is languidly strumming upon a stringed instrument in another world."

Bunny left the film industry in 1913 to return to the theater to perform his comedy routine at Hammerstein's Victoria Theater in New York City. In 1914, Bunny took an eight-week leave to tour with his show *Bunny in Funnyland,* which garnered rave reviews like this one published in Variety, "One of the best kids shows that has come this way for some time." Even with good reviews, the show failed, and Bunny was forced to give up the tour and produced *The John Bunny Show* at the Bronx Opera House. The reviews were unmerciful; one reported writing:

> *"Funny Bunny eh? At a nickel a throw to see the screen star in his silent antics, perhaps the billing is appropriate, but at a dollar per copy to see him at the Bronx opera house cavorting around with a mediocre company of mixed talent, presenting a brand of entertainment that forcibly suggests memories of a one-night-stand tabloid, it's a bit pathetic.*
>
> *And duly apologizing for the time-worn wheeze, let it be early recorded that as a star of the speaking stage, Funny Bunny is one of the best studio actors extant..."*

Bunny returned home to Los Angeles and was scheduled to begin working once again for Vitagraph in October 1915. Although outwardly, Bunny seemed healthy and happy, secretly, he was very ill suffering from Bright's disease, an affliction of the kidneys. This caused him severe pain and swelling due to water retention. Bunny died on April 26, 1915, in Brooklyn, New York, at the age of fifty-two.

John Bunny's funeral was held at the Elks Club House on West 43rd St in New York City at eight o'clock in the evening. Over one thousand people attended the service presided over by the officers of the lodge. The casket in the center of the room was surrounded by dozens of floral tributes sent by friends and colleagues from the legitimate stage and Vitagraph Studios. The pallbearers included William T. Rock, the president of Vitagraph, Samuel Speedon, Maurice Costello, Edward Scranton, George Baker, Van Dyck Brooks, Harry Morey, and Lee Beggs.

After the funeral and Masonic ritual, Bunny was taken to Evergreen Cemetery in Brooklyn, New York. A large headstone with the family name BUNNY adorns the gravesite. A small stone marking the actual burial site simply states John H. Bunny 1863 - 1915.

Sadly, within a few years, the contributions of Bunny were all but forgotten in the motion picture industry. The Bunny Theater in New York still stands as a tribute to Bunny, with two enormous bunnies adorning the outside of the building.

Very few of Bunny's films have lived on, and a few avid fans continue the legacy of a once-great man who has faded with time.

Our Gang

Our Gang, later known as the Little Rascals, was the brainchild of producer Hal Roach at the end of the 1930s. The premise of Our Gang followed the antics of a group of poor children through their day-to-day life in the 1930s in America. Roach came upon the idea after a painfully staged child audition, during which he looked out the window of his office across the street to a group of children playing on a construction site. They argued between themselves, trying to get the smallest child to give up a large stick to one of the bigger kids. He would not comply, but Roach was so entertained by the interaction and thought this premise might work on screen.

The series gained popularity with theater-going audiences in its first runs and maintained a continued success after the shorts were introduced to television, gaining additional audiences with Saturday morning kids programs. In addition to the show's popularity was the rumors of the Our Gang curse, causing the child actors who appeared on the show to die in tragic, premature deaths. While some of these rumors are true as to the actors' deaths, the "curse" of the series is considered a conspiracy theory by most.

The child actors were encouraged by director Robert F. McGowan to interact naturally rather than be staged like adult actors. This created a natural flow for the children, and the audience reaction to the short films was favorable from the beginning.

Roach and McGowan integrated whites and blacks, boys and girls, which was unheard of in 1930s cinema. This groundbreaking thinking moved Hollywood into a new age of filmmaking, with these children leading the way. A total of two hundred and twenty short films were made, with various actors being hired and fired from the cast when they began to mature past the child phase.

The first group of children to be recruited for the series consisted of Mary Korman, daughter of still photo cameraman Gene Korman, Mary's friend Mickey Daniels, Ernie "Sunshine Sammy" Morrison, and Allen "Farina" Hoskins. The shorts began filming during the silent era of film but quickly segwayed to talking pictures. By the 1930s, the faces changed, and the new generation of fresh faces became Our Gang. "Wheezer" Hutchins, Harry Spears, Jean Darling, and Mary Ann Jackson became the new stars with Farina, the only mainstay of the old guard.

Hutchins would be one of the first actors to die tragically, dying as the victim of a plane crash at the age of nineteen. Daniels also passed away early in his life of liver disease at the age of fifty-five.

With the advent of sound, the children were allowed to ad-lib most of the dialogue since very few of them could read. The first of the series talking was the classic *Small Talk,* in which the gang are orphans trying to get adopted. Wheezer gets adopted by a rich family, and the other children come to visit him in his new home, and chaos ensues.

With gaining popularity of the series, it also seemed to be a transitional period for the child actors. Within a year, they replaced most of the actors, and Norman "Chubby" Chaney, Jackie Cooper, "Froggy" Laughlin, and Matthew "Stymie" Beard became the new stars of the group.

Jackie Cooper was the first of the Our Gang stars to break out into motion pictures, leaving the series in 1931. At the age of nine, Cooper was nominated for the Academy Award® for his role in the film *Skippy* based on the comic strip of the same name. Cooper began acting at the age of three and was hired by Roach for the short films as an extra; within a year, he was cast in the starring roles for the series, gaining much attention from the studio executives.

By 1931, Cooper acted in a series of films opposite veteran actor Wallace Beery for Metro Goldwyn Mayer. *The Champ, The Bowery,* and *Treasure Island* were just a few of the motion pictures the duo made together. In a later interview, Cooper stated that he was terrified of Beery, saying the man hated children and undermined the boy's acting in these films.

Although most children struggled to transition from child to adult roles, Cooper managed with relative ease with starring roles in the television series *Hennessy* and *The People's Choice*. Cooper made another Hollywood transition from actor to studio executive during the 1960s, becoming vice president of programming for Screen Gems selling such programs as *Bewitched* and *Gidget*.

It was not until the 1970s and 1980s when Cooper returned to the screen as Daily Planet editor Perry White in *Superman* starring Christopher Reeves.

Throughout his life, Cooper maintained a hand in film and television from the advent of talking pictures. Cooper passed away on May 3, 2011, at the age of eighty-eight, still loved for his work as little Jackie Cooper.

Even with Cooper's fame, his costars would gain notoriety, not by their acting roles but by catching headlines in devastating accidents. "Froggy" died in a motor scooter accident at the age of sixteen, and "Chubby" passed away due to complications after a glandular surgery at the age of twenty-two. "Stymie" had trouble with the law, drugs, and alcohol throughout his teens and twenties but, in 1980, he recovered and toured the United States, giving his testimony to others struggling with addiction.

After Cooper's departure, Roach signed another new Our Gang child, George "Spanky" McFarland. McFarland's parents answered an ad in the trade papers looking for cute kids and sent a picture of their son. At the age of three, McFarland was a tag-along character, pestering the older kids to play with him or include him in their capers. McFarland had a knack for scene-stealing, and the studio insisted that they feature the toddler in more lead roles.

It was not until the introduction of sidekick Scotty Beckett in 1934 that Spanky would take on a more leadership role with the gang, being the idea man for the group.

Beckett would only be with the series from 1934 to 1935, leaving the series when his parents decided on a serious acting career for their son. Beckett worked infrequently, ending his career in his early twenties with a series of arrests and problems with drugs and alcohol. Beckett died at the age of twenty-four of a self-inflicted injury and was laid to rest at San Fernando Mission Cemetery in Los Angeles.

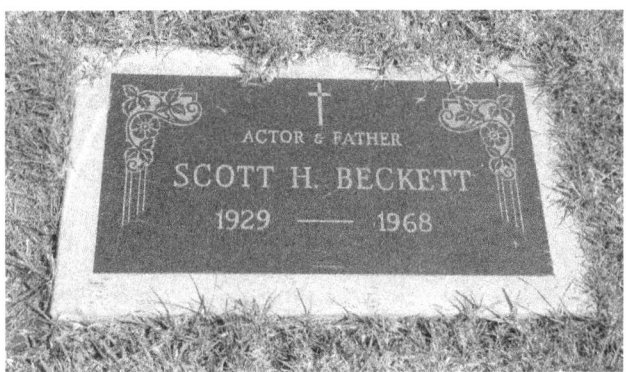

McFarland continued with the films for the next eleven years, eventually venturing out into other acting. Unfortunately for McFarland, Hollywood was only interested in typecasting him as the Spanky character, and he chose to go into the Air Force at the age of twenty-four. Once he left the armed forces, McFarland struggled to find work as an actor and finally took odd jobs until he was offered to host *The Spanky Show* in Tulsa, Oklahoma. The series ran the Our Gang shorts as McFarland gave the introductions. Creative differences with the station executives caused McFarland to leave the show, and, once again, he struggled to find work. Becoming a salesman, McFarland would sell furniture, electronics, appliances, and wine but ultimately became the national sales director for the Philco-Ford corporation.

During the 1990s, McFarland retired and traveled the country doing speaking engagements about his years with Roach and The Our Gang comedies. McFarland passed away on June 30, 1993, at the age of 64, and was quietly cremated.

Another of the major child stars of this time was Carl "Alfalfa" Switzer. Discovered by Roach at the age of eight, Switzer and his brother were visiting relatives in California when they toured the studio and entered the commissary where Roach was lunching. The boys put on an impromptu performance, and Roach hired them both on the spot.

In 1935, the brothers were cast in their first short *Beginners Luck,* with Alfalfa singing off-key in an amateur contest with his brother accompanying him in the act. Within a year, Switzer was one of the featured child stars of the series, usurping McFarland's popularity. The two boys got along well, but the fathers fought for years over billing and screen time. Switzer became difficult to work with as he loved to play dangerous pranks on set. One infamous prank caused serious injury to costar McFarland when he placed fish hooks in McFarland's pants, causing severe cuts. Another well-documented prank was his tendency to urinate on the studio lights before anyone would come on the set. Once the lights became hot, the stench would become unbearable, and they would lose valuable shooting time when the set would have to be cleared.

By 1940, the series came to a close, and Switzer tried in earnest to find work, appearing in *It's a Wonderful Life* with Jimmy Stewart and *Going my Way* with Bing Crosby. By 1946, Switzer was performing in *The Gas House Kids* series, a poor man's Bowery Boys, in an attempt to continue working.

As an adult, Hollywood typecast the young man. The frustration of his dying career, coupled with financial difficulties caused the Switzer family to move to Kansas, where he ultimately took a job breeding hunting dogs.

In January 1959, Switzer borrowed a hunting dog from a friend Moses "Bud" Stintz, and the dog disappeared. Switzer posted a fifty-dollar reward for the dog and received a call from someone claiming to have the dog. Switzer arranged a meeting to return the dog and, not having the money, paid the man thirty-five dollars in cash and twenty-five dollars' worth of alcohol. Switzer returned the dog to his friend.

Several days later, while drinking with friends, Switzer decided that Stintz owed him the $50.00 and went to his home to collect the money. Stintz opened his front door after Switzer pounded on it for several minutes. Switzer entered drunk and raging with anger, demanding his money. Rumors swirled that Switzer pulled a knife on the man threatening to kill him. As Switzer rushed Stintz, he pulled a gun and shot Switzer in the groin in self-defense.

Stintz was absolved of all responsibility for the crime, and Switzer's death went unnoticed by Hollywood. A footnote appeared in the Los Angeles Times, the headline taken by the death of movie mogul Cecil B. DeMille who died the same day. Switzer was buried at Hollywood

Forever Cemetery in Los Angeles next to his father, the simple headstone decorated with a hunting dog.

The female lead who caused most of the arguments between McFarland and Switzer was the lovely Darla Hood.

Hood began singing and dancing as soon as she could walk. At the tender age of three, Hood's mother took her to casting agent Joe Rivkin in New York, and he signed her to a contract with Roach to appear in the Our Gang comedies. The coquettish blonde later had her hair dyed brunette and enchanted star-eyed love Alfalfa, who fought valiantly for her against bully rival Butch and rich kid Waldo.

Along with her good looks, Hood delighted audiences with her singing capabilities, fondly remembered for her version of *I'm in the Mood for Love* in the short *The Pinch Singer*.

Once the Our Gang series ended, Hood continued singing and attended Fairfax high school in Los Angeles. Immediately after graduation, Hood was signed to the Blackout's singing group managed by Ken Murray. She continued her success with the group and, in the 1950s, she toured the nightclub circuit with Murray.

Hood continued great success for the next two decades, performing on television programs and doing voice-over work for television commercials.

One of the only child actors to maintain success throughout her life, tragedy struck the young woman when she went into the hospital for a minor operation and contracted acute hepatitis, died suddenly of a heart attack at the age of forty-seven. Hood was buried at Hollywood Forever Cemetery in Los Angeles in the Abbey of the Psalms mausoleum near costar Carl Switzer.

In addition to the principal characters, two of the more popular actors of the series would be William "Buckwheat" Thomas and Eugene "Porky" Lee. Although not considered stars of the series, "Buckwheat" remains one of the most endearing characters being spoofed by Eddie Murphy on *Saturday Night Live*.

Thomas's character became the center of much controversy during the series run, being typecast as the pica ninny stereotype with braided hair, oversized clothes, and boots. The character evolved to the striped shirt, suspenders, and overgrown hairdo later, but still, Thomas would become the ever-present go-to man for Spanky. Thomas continued to defend his work years later, stating Roach treated him as an equal to the white kids on the set and was always respected on set as a professional.

In 1954, Thomas joined the United States Army, being awarded a National Defense Service Medal and a Good Conduct Medal. After his service, Thomas had no interest in going back to Hollywood but began a new career in Hollywood as a film lab technician editing finished film.

Thomas passed away of a heart attack on October 10, 1980, and was buried in a private ceremony at Inglewood Park Cemetery in Whittier, California.

In 1990, the news journalist show *20/20* aired a segment with a man claiming to be Thomas working as a grocery bagger in Arizona. The imposter was exposed immediately after the show aired when McFarland contacted the producers to prove Thomas's had died ten years prior. The show corrected the error the next week, but the producer resigned his position, and the studio settled a lawsuit with the son of Thomas without media attention.

The Porky character was introduced in 1935 as the sidekick to the ever-present Buckwheat character and soon had his own catchphrase, "Otay." Throughout the years, this phrase has been attributed to Thomas mistakenly. Originally, Lee was cast as Spanky's little brother, but this relationship was dropped after one episode. Lee appeared in forty-one comedies over four years.

In 1939, Lee grew several inches in just a few months, making him as tall as McFarland. The studio released Lee and replaced him with child actor Mickey Gubitosi who later changed his name to Robert Blake and found success as *Baretta* in the 1970s. Blake gained much notoriety in the early 2000s when he was arrested and charged with the murder of his wife, Bonnie Lee Bakley. He was ultimately acquitted and retired from the spotlight following the lengthy court case.

The Our gang series later changed to *The Little Rascals* when MGM studios took over and continue to this day to be a source of nostalgia for those remembering a simple time when children's imaginations could entertain and charm without big-budget spectacles.

Charley Chase

While Charley Chase was not considered in the same league as the likes of Charlie Chaplin and Buster Keaton, Chase and his comedy silent films are highly regarded as some of the greatest works of the silent era.

Chase was born Charles Parrot just before the turn of the century in Baltimore, Maryland, the son of Charles and Blanche Parrott, a vaudeville family. Chase's father, a heavy drinker, died of a heart attack in 1903, leaving the family without the means to survive. Chase worked as a street corner entertainer and took odd jobs to support his mother and brother James. Soon, Chase began performing in local saloons and became somewhat of a celebrity around the neighborhood. By 1910, Chase hit the big time and began touring the country with a Vaudeville troupe. For the next two years, Chase performed nightly, perfecting his comedy routine to the delight of audiences.

While Chase was talented, he was also highly anxious, having a piece of string to manipulate between his fingers to calm his nerves. If there were hecklers in the audience, Chase would be thrown off and sometimes leave the stage in the middle of a performance.

Chase finally decided to try his hand at acting in motion pictures and headed for Hollywood in 1912. Chase found work with the Al Christie filmmaking unit at Universal Studio but felt working with the great Mack Sennett would be better for his career and moved quickly over to Keystone Studio. In the beginning, Chase worked in bit parts with great stars like Roscoe Arbuckle and Charlie Chaplin. While Keystone did not use Chase as a full-time actor, Chase learned the technical side of film making, eventually becoming a director, and left Keystone in 1917 to direct two-reel features for the Fox Film Corporation. This proved to be a short-lived partnership as Chase left Fox within one year to work with Paramount studios.

Chase had made a name for himself with the comedy films he was directing, and the studios were clamoring for more Chase films. In 1920, Hal Roach Studio benefited from a partnership agreement with Chase, having been made director-general of the studio and supervising the entire production process.

Chase enjoyed working behind the camera but was persuaded to step in front of the camera in 1923 when Roach lost mega star Harold Lloyd and needed a replacement. Chase changed his name from Parrott to Chase and began working as an actor once more.

With Leo Carey's help, Chase learned the fine art of characterization on the screen rather than the outrageous gags and physical comedy he used in his stage act. He played the part of the good-natured, dapper man getting into embarrassing situations. *His Wooden Wedding, Innocent Husbands, Mighty Like a Moose,* and *Crazy Like a Fox* considered to date to be some of his best work. In addition to his acting, Chase was the director, editor, and writer of most of his films. He was using his given name Charles Parrot for his directing credits.

With the advent of talking pictures, Chase transitioned easily using his fine baritone singing voice in several of his talking pictures. Chase quickly became one of the most prolific actors of the sound era, one of his greatest accomplishments being *The Pip from Pittsburgh* costarring Thelma Todd.

Chase refused to transition to the full-length feature films being produced at Hal Roach Studios. Chase made one attempt with the genre, but the production was plagued with both technical and artistic issues. The film was finally cut down to two reels before its release, and Chase was dismissed from Hal Roach Studios in 1936 due to the studio phasing out the two-reel comedies.

The next year, Chase began working with Columbia Pictures and made a series of two-reel comedies as well as producing and directing up-and-coming film stars like Laurel and Hardy.

Even with all of the fame and success, Chase was plagued with drinking problems for most of his career. Younger brother James was a known drug addict, and Chase refused to enable his addiction by giving him money. James died of heart failure, and Chase felt responsible for his brother's death. His drinking became more profound during this time, and doctors warned Chase that his health was failing due to the large amounts of alcohol he was consuming.

Chase disregarded the advice, and within months of his brother's death, Chase suffered a fatal heart attack on June 20, 1940, and died at the age of forty-six.

Charley Chase was buried at Forest Lawn Memorial Park in Glendale, California. A simple granite stone marks the grave Charley Chase 1893 - 1940.

James Finlayson

Known as "Mr. Double Take," James Finlayson is best known as the straight man to the team of Laurel and Hardy, but this is only a small part of the broad spectrum of work performed during Finlayson's long career in the Silent and talking Comedies. Destine to make people laugh; Finlayson was a genuine star with a body of work that stands even today as some of the greatest comedy work in film history.

Born in Scotland, Finlayson was raised by his mother and father in the province of Larbert, Stirlingshire. The exact date of his birth is shady, with Finlayson never being direct about the date.

Finlayson was an apprentice to his father in the ironworks industry but turned his back on this work and went to college to study business. This direction of his life was also short-lived as Finlayson dropped out of college after meeting actor John Clyde and falling in love with acting. He appeared in theaters in and around London for several years, honing his craft and learning from the more established actors of the time. In 1911, Finlayson arrived in the United States, settling in New York. One of Finlayson's first roles was in the West End stage production of *Bunty Pulls the Strings,* followed by *The Great Game.* Finlayson reprised his role in *Bunty Pull the Strings* on Broadway, and the play was a smash hit, playing for the next eighteen months to packed theaters. Finlayson toured with the company here in the U.S. and performed in Vaudeville in the sketch of *The Concealed Bed* until 1916.

Finlayson decided it was time to try the movies and decided to move to Hollywood. Finlayson met director Mack Sennett, and Sennett cast Finlayson as one of the original Keystone Cops in the early silent films. After his three-year contract expired, Finlayson decided to move on and not renew with Sennett or Keystone Studios.

Finlayson wanted more from his career in the movies and signed a four-year contract with Hal Roach Studio in the mid-1920s. Finlayson was paired with the comedy duo of Laurel and Hardy, getting equal billing with the pair, but the studio decided a trio would not draw the box office as well as a twosome. Finlayson became the heavy in the Laurel & Hardy films; the antagonistic relationship became an integral part of the films. Altogether, the men made thirty-three films together.

Another of Finlayson's most memorable films was the Our Gang short film *Mush and Milk*, in which he and Spanky McFarland match wits in a comical phone conversation in which McFarland wins. Finlayson appeared in a total of six Our Gang features during his tenure with Roach.

The trademark mustache worn by Finlayson was a prop; the actor feeling no need to grow one of his own. Several of his films before and after his partnership with Hal Roach show the actor without facial hair, causing him to be unrecognized in some of his films. Another of Finlayson's trademarks was his drawn-out "Doooooooooooo" when he was foiled by a nemesis. This later became a source of inspiration for Homer Simpson's character in the long-running animated series *The Simpson's* as a nod to Finlayson.

After his association with Roach came to an end, Finlayson continued working as a freelance actor with several other studios and made another nineteen pictures while in Hollywood. In his later years, Finlayson moved to England and made several pictures while living abroad.

With age, Finlayson slowed down and retired from performing, moving back to Los Angeles. He suffered a fatal heart attack on October 9, 1953, and was found by good friend and actress Stephanie Insall when she arrived at his home after he did not meet her for breakfast.

The obituary that ran in the Hollywood Reports was brief and unmemorable.

"Funeral services will be held today for Jimmy Finlayson (86), one of the original Keystone Kops, at 3 p.m. at Pierce Bros., Hollywood. The actor, who was also heavy in two reelers, died in his sleep at his Hollywood home."

Attending Finlayson's funeral included fellow Keystone Kops Hank Mann, Billy Bevan, Snub Pollard, and Tom Kennedy. Mack Sennett himself was also there paying tribute to the great funny man.

Finlayson was cremated after the service, and his remains were given to his family.

Al Jolson

Dubbed the world's greatest entertainer during his heyday, Al Jolson set the entertainment world on fire with his singing, dancing, and acting both on stage and in motion pictures.

Born Asa Yoelson in the Jewish village of Srednik in Lithuania. The exact date of Jolson's birth is a mystery due to the lack of records, but Jolson chose May 26, 1886, to celebrate the day of his birth. The youngest of five children, Jolson grew up in a poverty-stricken village; his father, a rabbi and cantor in the synagogue, and could not support his family. In 1891 Jolson's father packed his bags and left for America unaccompanied to begin securing the funds to bring his family over to join him. His wife and children boarded a ship to the United States three years later in 1894, and the family settled in Washington

D.C. Tragedy struck the family when Jolson's mother died suddenly not long after arriving in America.

Jolson was grief-stricken at the loss of his mother and withdrew into himself to protect himself from the pain. Fate stepped in the next year when Jolson met performer Al Reeves who encouraged the young man to begin learning the art of stage performing. Jolson and his brother Harry began singing on street corners to earn enough money to attend the theater where Jolson would sit in the darkness and study the actors on stage.

In 1902, Jolson got his first job in the theater but not as a performer. Jolson worked as an usher for the Walter L. Main Circus, but Main heard Jolson's singing one day and gave him a job in the sideshow. Luck was not on Jolson's side as the circus had to close permanently within a few months. This curse followed Jolson as he got his next job in a burlesque house, and the show closed soon after he began performing. Jolson called his brother Hirsch who was already working in Vaudeville, and the two boys performed on national tours. They soon met Vaudevillian Joe Palmer, and the duo became a trio. While performing in a Brooklyn theater, Jolson decided to take a huge gamble one night and come out on the stage to sing in black face. The crowd loved the act, and Jolson decided to use the makeup every night, imitating a black man on the stage. This type of performance was quite common at the time but fell out of favor over the years. Harry left the act when he and his brother argued about the care of wheelchair-bound Palmer. Palmer and Jolson continued touring after losing their third partner, but the magic was gone, and they went their separate ways in 1905.

Jolson settled in San Francisco after the devastating earthquake and found much success on the west coast. Jolson married dancer Henrietta Keller while living in San Francisco and, by 1908, the couple moved back to New York. Jolson found that the move back east was a blessing as he met producer J.J. Shubert and was cast in the musical *La Belle Paree* at the Winter Garden Theater, working as a singer in black face once again. The show ran for one hundred and four performances, and Jolson became the toast of New York. His next show, *Vera Violetta,* found Jolson performing essentially the same act, but his popularity with audiences grew just the same. During his time on Broadway, Jolson created the tag line he used throughout his career "You ain't heard nothin' yet!" Audiences heard the line at the Winter Garden theater for the next seven years when Lee Shubert offered Jolson a thousand dollars a week to work with the show exclusively. Jolson's songs also became his trademark, with *My Mammy, Swanee,* and *Rock-a-bye your baby with a Dixie Melody* becoming national hits.

By 1916 Jolson's salary was doubled, making him one of the highest-paid entertainers of the era. In 1918, Henrietta filed for divorce from her husband when she discovered his many infidelities backstage.

In the 1920s, it seemed Jolson could do nothing wrong on the stage. Every show became a smash hit, and Jolson was a superstar. Shubert built a new theater and named it Jolson's Fifty-ninth Street Theater. During the opening night at the new theater, Jolson found himself turning a page in his life when he developed paralyzing stage fright.

Jolson walked up and down the street, trying to calm his nerves for hours before showtime but found himself backstage shaking and sweating while begging the stage manager not to bring the curtain up. When he would not take the stage, his brother Harry literally shoved Jolson out of the wings, and Jolson performed thirty-seven curtain calls that night. Jolson could not explain the fear later but went on night after night to thunderous applause. He kept buckets in both wings of the stage just in case his nerve got the better of him from then on.

Charles Darnton in the *New York Evening World* wrote this about Jolson:

"I don't mind going on record as saying that he is one of the few instinctively funny men on our stage. Everything he touches turns to fun. To watch him is to marvel at his humorous vitality. He is the old-time minstrel man turned to modern account. With a song, a word, or even a suggestion, he calls forth spontaneous laughter. And here you have the definition of a born comedian."

In 1922 Jolson met chorus girl Ethel Delmar and courted the young girl, marrying her in July 1922. It was not long after the marriage that Ethel found herself alone for months and began drinking heavily to numb the loneliness. When Jolson developed bronchitis in 1925, he took an extended vacation with his wife and found out she was an alcoholic. Jolson resumed the neglect of his marriage and returned to the stage after a brief hiatus. By 1926 the couple divorced, and Ethel continued to be supported by Jolson for the rest of her life.

While Jolson's star continued to rise on Broadway, he was offered a role in his first talking picture, *Mammy's Boy*, directed by D.W. Griffith. Many think his next film was Jolson's first, but this obscure film still lives and is a testament to the burgeoning talking pictures.

Finally, in 1927, Jolson was offered the lead role on a new motion picture that changed the face of film-making forever. *The Jazz Singer* became the first talking picture in wide release, with Jolson performing his classic hit songs to a mesmerized audience. The film was considered a novelty by rival studios, but soon they found that if they wanted to stay in business, sound pictures were the way to move forward. The premiere allowed the movie-going public to hear for the first time Jolson utter the phrase, "Wait a minute, wait a minute, you ain't heard nothin' yet." Warner Brothers offered Jolson his next film, *The Singing Fool*, in 1928, followed by *Say it With Songs* in 1930.

With his success on stage and in films, Jolson set his sights on singer-dancer Ruby Keeler for his next romance. Keeler was involved with legendary gangster Johnny Costello, but Jolson was unimpressed, showering Keeler with gifts. The pair married in 1928 after Jolson gave Keeler a gift of one million dollars. The couple honeymooned in Europe, but upon their return to the United States, Jolson forgot about his bride and went back to his first love, the stage. Keeler continued her own career and stayed in the marriage as a convenience.

In the 1930s, Jolson's audience became bored with the same songs on stage and in his films. His next show, *The Wonder Bar* was a flop and closed after ten weeks. Jolson suffered from throat ailments and missed numerous performances causing theater owners to change their minds about Jolson's staying power. Jolson's film career became stagnant as well with many box office bombs.

Never the type to give up easily, Jolson went back to radio and worked as a guest on several of the top shows of the late 1930s. While Jolson's career was fading, Keeler's career was soaring, which caused the marriage to become difficult with the competition. Jolson became verbally abusive to Keeler, and she filed for divorce in 1939.

During World War II, Jolson contacted the top military brass begging to go abroad to entertain the troops and became the first entertainer to perform on international military bases. He worked tirelessly touring the United States and Europe singing the songs he made classic for millions of soldiers for the next two wars.

Jolson became a household name once again when Columbia Pictures Harry Cohn produced *The Al Jolson Story*. Jolson was too old to play himself in the film, so they hired veteran actor Larry Parks to play Jolson. A young Scotty Beckett played Jolson as a boy in the film. Jolson recorded all of the vocals for the film and appeared in one scene singing and dancing in a wide-angle camera shot. The film was a huge success, and Jolson made a fortune with a percentage of the box office and recording rights. His career was on the rise once again, keeping him busy in radio and recording new albums.

On October 23, 1950, Jolson was preparing for *The Bing Crosby* radio show resting in his hotel room at the St. Francis hotel in San Francisco with friends. During their card game, Jolson complained of indigestion and went to bed. The hotel doctor was called, and Jolson joked with the physician about his symptoms. Suddenly Jolson felt his pulse and spoke his final words, "Oh, I'm going." Jolson died at the age of sixty-four. That evening Broadway dimmed its lights to honor Jolson.

The funeral for Jolson became the biggest memorial in recorded history, with over twenty thousand people in attendance. Actor George Jessel gave a tearful eulogy stating:

> *"And not only has the entertainment world lost its king, but we cannot cry, "The king is dead, long live the king!" For there is no one to hold his scepter. Those of us who tarry behind are but pale imitators, mere princelings."* . . . Jolson

was synonymous with victory – at the race track, at the ball game, at anything that he participated in, he would say, "I had the winner, ha, ha, why didn't you ask me?" This was not in bravado alone: this was the quintessence of optimism. Whatever game you're in, whatever game you play, feel like you are the winner."

Jolson's body was buried in a temporary grave until almost one year later when his widow had him move to a black marble outdoor tomb below an enormous gazebo with a bronze statue of Jolson on one knee adorning the memorial sitting atop a two-story waterfall.

Chapter 2
From the big screen to the small screen 1940 – 1950

From the silent films to the talkies, Hollywood continued to grow with bigger and better entertainment for the audiences that flocked to theaters to watch their favorite comedians on the screen.

At the end of the 1940s, a new menace in entertainment came on the scene, with televisions popping up in homes across the nation. Suddenly, people found they could stay in the comfort of their homes to laugh along with their favorite characters instead of going to the movies for their amusement. Comedy once again would adapt to the new medium of television, steaming situation comedies every evening to the delight of the at-home viewers.

A style of humor came to play with a generation of comedians taking cues from the big screen and adapting them for a more casual audience.

Milton Berle

One of the first stars of television, Milton Berle, became the best-known comedian of the 1950s known as Uncle Milty or Mr. Television. Coming into the homes of millions of viewers each week, Berle ushered America into a new era of entertainment in the golden age of television.

Berle was born Milton Berlinger in Harlem, New York, just after the turn of the twentieth century. Berle began his creative talent at the age of five when he won a local amateur talent contest. In an interview with Berle in 2000, he stated,

"My mother recognized I had talent and she said it was all for Milton. She knew what she wanted for me and took me around to all the auditions. She would find out ahead of time what kind of kid they wanted (i.e.: Ragamuffin, tough kid,

little lord Fauntleroy, etc.) and she would spend her last nickel to dress me up and coach me what to say to the director. I was the bread winner and she poured all her energies into me."

In 1914, not long after his debut on the stage, Berle was cast as a child actor in the New Jersey production of *The Perils of Pauline*, a feature-length motion picture directed by Louis J. Gasnier and starring Pearl White and Paul Panzer.

In Berle's biography *Milton Berle: An Autobiography,* he talks about several other feature films he was cast in like, *Bunny's Little Brother, Tess of the Storm Country, Birthright,* and *Rebecca of Sunnybrook Farm* starring Mary Pickford. While Berle claimed to appear in dozens of films during this time, the claims have been disputed by many of his contemporaries. The truth as to his appearances in these films is lost to time as there is no concrete evidence proving the truth of Berle's statements.

In 1916, Berle was enrolled in the Professional Children's School, a privately-owned college preparatory school founded in New York City for young performers. At the age of twelve, Berle was cast in the show *Florodora*. This role put Berle on the track to a career that continued to enchant audiences for the next five decades. The show was such a hit that it went to Broadway, and Berle was given the exposure he needed to be one of the most recognized entertainers in the United States.

Throughout the 1920s, Berle appeared as a standup comedian, tried his hand at songwriting, and appeared in a test program for the new experimental medium of television.

In the mid-1930s, Berle appeared regularly on *The Rudy Vallee Hour* and *The Gillette Original Community Sing* radio shows. Berle continued success with radio, appearing as a regular guest star on most of the top-rated programs of the decade as well as maintaining his show to record listening audiences.

By 1947, Berle was given his own show *Milton Berle Show*. A popular hit, Berle was approached by Texaco to headline *The Texaco Star Theater* show in 1948. Berle agreed and signed a contract with Texaco. He later stated in an interview, "It was the best radio show I ever did, a hell of a funny variety show."

The next year, Texaco decided to move the show from radio to television, continuing their association with Berle as one of four rotating hosts. By the fall of 1948, Berle was declared solo host and star of the show. The new television show was a success with audiences every Tuesday night, with over eighty percent of the television viewing audience tuning in each week. Berle appeared every week in a different costume and was known for his wild getups, even dressing as a woman complete with a sequin evening gown, long blonde wig, and poorly applied makeup. The only prop Berle ever used on the show was his ever-present cigar, which became a trademark for the comedian.

By the end of the 1940s, Berle was a bonafide star. Television sales skyrocketed, and "Mr. Television" was born. NBC signed Berle with an unprecedented thirty-year contract to ensure they would continue their present success and not lose their top commodity to another broadcast rival.

While NBC enjoyed their triumph with "Uncle Milty," as Berle referred to himself with the younger audience, they had no way of knowing that the climate of television would change or that the viewing audiences would tire of the repeated antics week after week.

In 1947, Berle founded The Friars Club along with contemporaries Bing Crosby, George Jessel, Jimmy Durante, and Robert Taylor. The club was a private male membership for actors to offer good-natured roasts of fellow celebrities. Berle enjoyed the club as a way to escape from the limelight and take pleasure in camaraderie with other celebrities.

Over the next few years, ratings continued to fall, and Texaco pulled their sponsorship of the show that Berle had made famous. Buick, the car manufacturer, picked up the show as a sponsor but only stayed with Berle for two seasons when they could not regain the previous popularity. As viewership continued to plunge, Berle was reduced to hosting a bowling program and finally left television to pursue other entertainment venues.

After television, Berle appeared in the booming new oasis of Las Vegas. Berle was an instant headliner, packing audiences into the biggest casinos with his stand-up comedy act.

Berle was known throughout show business as a collector of jokes. He claimed to amass several million in his collection, mostly stealing them from other comedians. At one memorable event, Bob Hope stated Berle, "Never heard a joke he didn't steal." Jack Benny enjoyed joking at Berle's expense, claiming, "When you take a joke away from Milton Berle, it's not stealing, it's repossessing."

Berle also stretched his acting ability and appeared in several motion pictures during the 1960s. Berle appeared with Marilyn Monroe in *Let's Make Love*, Virginia Mayo in *Always Leave them laughing,* and Woody Allen's *Broadway Danny Rose*. Berle proved to be a good dramatic actor and comic, earning great acclaim for his dramatic performances.

Berle made appearances on several of the top television shows of the 1960s, like *The Lucy Show* starring Lucille Ball, *The Jackie Gleason Show,* and *The Sonny and Cher Comedy Hour.* Always the unforgettable guest, Berle would repeatedly attempt to upstage the star and get the last laugh. Later in his career, Berle appeared as a guest on the *Saturday Night Live* show as a guest host. Berle attempted to use his classic television shtick to upstage the troupe and monopolize the screen time. Producer Lauren Michaels found Berle difficult to work with and banned Berle from ever appearing on the show in future episodes.

While Berle enjoyed decades of success and worked clean for his entire career, the man off-screen was a different animal entirely. Berle was known for using offensive language in his business and social dealings, never filtering his speech. He was unaware of the inappropriate nature of his dialog. While criticizing other comedians for their use of foul language on stage, Berle never considered the foul language he used in everyday life off-limits.

Another legacy Berle left was his need to let everyone in show business know that he was endowed with an enormous penis. Rumors traveled throughout Hollywood that Berle was exceedingly endowed physically, and he enjoyed the company of many of the top female stars.

In his later years, it was rumored that, on the SNL set, Berle took out his member and showed it to writer Alan Zweibel. Zweibel stated in an interview:

> *"He just takes out this— this anaconda. He lays it on the table and I'm looking into this thing, right? I'm looking into the head of Milton Berle's dick. It was enormous. It was like a pepperoni. And he goes, 'What do you think of the boy?' And I'm looking right at it, and I go, 'Oh, it's really, really nice.'"*

Regardless of his persona off stage, Berle was highly respected as one of the pioneers of comedy. In 1984 Berle was honored as one of the first seven celebrities inducted into the Television Academy Hall of Fame and, in 1991, became the first entertainer inducted into the International Comedy Hall of Fame.

Berle suffered a stroke in December 1999 but continued working on television with guest appearances on several of the more popular shows like *Beverly Hills 90210* and *The Nanny*.

In April 2001, Berle announced that he was diagnosed with colon cancer, but his wife stated publicly that the tumor was growing slowly and would take ten years to affect her husband. Clearly, Berle was affected more than they realized, passing away less than one year later on March 27, 2002, in Los Angeles, California, the same day of the passing of actor Dudley Moore and writer Billy Wilder.

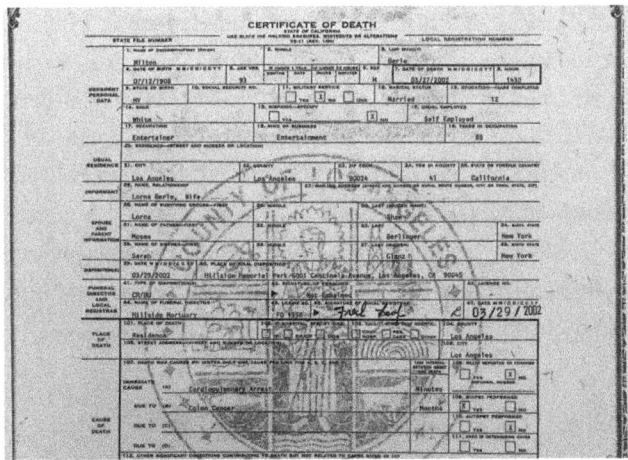

The funeral service for Milton Berle was made public and held at Hillside Memorial Park in Culver City, California, on April 1, 2002. Several eulogies were given by great comedians like Don Rickles, Red Buttons, Jan Murray, Buddy Hackett, and Larry Gelbart.

Also present at the service were son-in-law Richard Moll, Actress Audrey Meadows and comedy legend Sid Cesar.

Private interment followed the service at Hillside Memorial Park. Berle's original burial plan was to be buried next to his first wife at Mt. Sinai Memorial Park in Los Angeles, but his second wife, Lorna, decided to change the arrangements and have him interred at Hillside Memorial Park.

Milton Berle lays in state in an outdoor mausoleum with a bronze plate on the crypt front that reads, "You filled our lives with laughter and love."

George Burns

The cigar-smoking legend of stage, screen, and television, George Burns made a name for himself solo and with his wife, Gracie Allen, with a career spanning seventy years. The diminutive, gravelly-voiced star, loved by fans and colleagues alike as the straight man of Burns and Allen's comedy duo.

George Burns was born Nathan Birnbaum on January 20, 1896, the ninth of twelve children born to Louis and Dorothy Birnbaum in New York City. When Burns was eight years old, his father died in the great influenza epidemic of 1903, leaving his wife and children destitute. It was then that Burns began working to help support the family doing odd jobs like shining shoes and selling newspapers. Burns found steady work making syrup in a factory with several other children. The work was laborious, and the children bored easily. Burns and four of the children began singing to pass the time and soon developed four-part harmony. When the workers began acknowledging the singing, Burns decided the group should start singing professionally and give up the syrup business.

In an interview with Burns, he was quoted as saying, "We called ourselves the Peewee Quartet. We started out singing on ferryboats, in saloons, in brothels, and on street corners. We'd put our hats down for donations. Sometimes the customers threw something in the hats. Sometimes they took something out of the hats. Sometimes they took the hats."

Burns quit school in the fourth grade to pursue a full-time career in Vaudeville, learning to dance, sing, act, roller skate, and practically anything else to entertain an audience. Burns worked with several partners during this time but was unable to find the right chemistry with anyone until 1923, when he met a young performer by the name of Gracie Allen.

The Burns and Allen act/combo was an instant success on the Vaudeville circuit. A reliable team, they were able to fill in for any act that would be absent for their performance, and their ratings soared. When the duo finally appeared at the legendary Palace Theater on Broadway in New York, they knew they had hit the big time.

At the onset of the pairing, Burns tried to be the duo's funny man but quickly flipped the arrangement, giving Gracie the laughs as she connected better with the audience as the scatterbrained, illogical woman. While the pair toured together, they were not a couple; Allen was committed to another man. Burns found himself falling in love with Allen, but she refused him several times. It was rumored that Burns carried a ring in his pocket while they traveled, hoping she would change her mind and accept his marriage proposal. It was Christmas 1925 that Allen finally realized that she, too, was in love with her comedy partner, and the two married on January 7, 1926, in Cleveland, Ohio, while on tour.

Burns and Allen continued touring together but eventually found themselves reinventing the act when they were offered a chance to appear on the *Guy Lombardo* radio show as a comedy team. They took the offer and soon found themselves being presented with their own show in 1932.

The duo enjoyed continued success throughout their years on the radio, but eventually, audience tastes began to change, and Burns had to look once again toward the future.

In 1950, Burns, now 54, decided the twosome would take the act from radio to television with *The George Burns and Gracie Allen Show*. CBS picked up the popular couple along with performer comedian Jack Benny. *The Burns and Allen Show* showcased a middle-aged couple with many of the same comedy techniques they used in their radio show. This did not work for the new format and was quickly changed to a routine, situation comedy, which the audiences adored.

At the same time, Burns and Allen were being invited into the homes of television viewers, Allen began having health problems. A heart ailment left her exhausted from the full-time filming schedule, and she wanted to retire but stayed on because she wanted to honor her commitment to Burns. The show ran from 1950 through 1958, with Burns and CBS finally omitting Allen from the show to convalesce. Burns tried valiantly to continue the show without Allen, but the show was canceled after one more year.

Allen passed away of a heart attack on August 27, 1964, after a long battle with heart disease. She was sixty-nine and had been Burns' wife and a sidekick for nearly 40 years. Burns was devastated after her death and would visit her crypt once a month to sit near Allen and talk to her about whatever was going on in his life at the time.

Burns, no longer performing himself, threw himself into producing television shows like *Mr. Ed, No Time for Sergeants,* and *Mona McClusky*. After a period of time, Burns began touring again, partnering with the likes of Carol Channing, Jane Russell, and Connie Haines. Burns also appeared in solo performances to sell-out crowds proving he could still pack them in.

In 1974, good friend Jack Benny was offered a role in a new film entitled *The Sunshine Boys* but turned it down due to his failing health. He told the studio to cast Burns in the role, and Burns won the Academy Award® that year for his performance of the ex-Vaudevillian Al Lewis. At eighty years old, Burns was the oldest person ever to win an Oscar in the history of the awards show until 1989, when Jessica Tandy won for *Driving Miss Daisy* at the age of eighty-one.

During the filming of *Sunshine Boys*, Benny passed away after suffering from pancreatic cancer. A tearful

Burns gave the eulogy for his long-time friend stating, "Jack was someone special to all of you but he was so special to me…I cannot imagine my life without Jack Benny and I will miss him so very much."

At the age of eighty, Burns' career was now on an upswing. In 1977, Burns was cast opposite singer John Denver in the role of God in the film *Oh, God!*. When Burns was asked why he took the role, he stated, "I was the closest to Him in age." The movie was a hit with audiences, and Burns reprised his omnipotent role for two sequels, *Oh, God Book II* and *Oh God, Your Devil,* where Burns played a dual role of God and the Devil.

Burns continued to work steadily with film and television roles well into his nineties as well as writing books. His final role was in the 1994 film *Radioland Murders,* starring as a one-hundred-year-old stand-up comedian.

In 1988, Burns received the Kennedy Center Honors and quipped that he had booked himself into the London Palladium and Caesars Palace for his one-hundredth birthday. When Burns was asked about his feelings on dying, he was quoted as saying, "I don't believe in dying… It's been done."

Burns continued to live his final years as a happily retired senior. He enjoyed excellent health until July 1994, when Burns fell in his bathtub and was forced to have surgery to remove fluid from his brain. From that time on, Burns never fully recouped his health; however, he celebrated his one-hundredth birthday on January 20, 1996, at his home, surrounded by friends and family.

Just over a month later, Burns passed away on March 9, 1996, of Cardiac Arrest at his home in Beverly Hills. Burns enjoyed his life but stated that he looked forward to death because Gracie would be there waiting for him in heaven.

Burns' funeral was held at the Wee Kirk o' the Heather chapel at Forest Lawn Memorial Park in Glendale, California, on March 12, 1996. Burns was dressed by his valet, who had worked for Burns some forty-plus years. Burns was dressed in a navy-blue suit with a pale blue shirt and red tie. His toupee was in place, along with his wedding ring and the watch that had been a gift from Allen during their marriage. Three cigars were placed in the breast pocket, his car keys, and three one-hundred-dollar bills just in case a card game broke out.

The New York Times ran the following tearful obituary for the legendary comedian:

George Burns, Straight Man And Ageless Wit, Dies at 100
By ALBIN KREBS
Published: March 10, 1996

George Burns, the cigar-puffing comedian who was the best comic "straight man" of his time in a partnership with the brilliantly scatterbrained Gracie Allen, and who began a solo career when he was nearly 80, died yesterday. He was 100 years old and his career in show business lasted 93 years.

He died at his home in Beverly Hills, Calif., said his manager, Irving Fein.

The diminutive, gravel-voiced Mr. Burns, delivering doses of his dry humor and occasionally breaking into a fragment of some long-forgotten vaudeville ditty, all the while savoring a huge cigar, was a beloved figure to several generations of Americans. He not only survived but triumphed in vaudeville, radio, television, nightclubs, records, books and movies. Even as he aged, he seemed ageless.

When he was well into his 90's, Mr. Burns announced with his customary brio that he had arranged to celebrate his 100th birthday, on Jan. 20, 1996, with an engagement at the London Palladium. That being the case, he noted, he could not possibly die -- "I'm booked," he explained.

After the funeral service, Burns was laid to rest with his beloved Gracie in the Freedom Mausoleum at Forest Lawn Memorial park in Glendale, California. The bronze marker was changed to read "Gracie Allen and George Burns, Together Again." It was said that one of Burns's last requests was that Allen get top billing on their crypt.

Lucille Ball

The beautiful red-headed comedienne who became an international star of stage, screen, and television delighted audiences with her zany calamities for over forty years.

Lucille Desiree Ball was born the oldest of two children to Desiree and Henry Ball in Jamestown, New York, on August 6, 1911.

Childhood for Ball was troubled with lack of money, which required her father to relocate the family to Detroit, Michigan, so that he could work as a telephone lineman. When Ball was almost four years old, her father was struck with typhoid fever and died, leaving the family destitute.

Ball's mother was still pregnant with Ball's younger brother, so she packed up and moved back to Jamestown, where she quickly met and married Ed Peterson. Peterson did not care for children and convinced the young mother to leave the children with his family while the pair went off to Detroit. Ball recalled in her memoirs that the family had little money, and she even went without school pencils due to lack of funds.

Finally, at the age of eleven, Ball was reunited with her mother, and the family was whole once again. Ball begged her mother to let her attend the New York City drama school at the age of fifteen, and her mother agreed.

Ball attended school with future star Bette Davis, considered one of the most talented students. Ball was shy, and the school felt the family was wasting their time by allowing their daughter to continue pursuing acting. Despite the school's reservations, Ball continued working on her acting and, by 1927, was modeling for fashion designer Hattie Carnegie and Chesterfield Cigarettes.

Ball suffered from a bout of rheumatoid arthritis, causing her to move back to Jamestown for a time, but she recovered and continued working towards a career in show business.

By the early 1930s, Ball had moved to Hollywood and dyed her hair blonde to make herself more appealing to casting directors. Ball worked as a model and appeared as a bit player in a few films. With the 1937 production of Stage Door, Ball began being noticed by the studio heads as she was given larger speaking parts with notables Ginger Rogers and Katharine Hepburn. In 1939 Ball was one of the hundreds of hopeful actresses vying for the part of Scarlett O'Hara in *Gone With the Wind* but was rejected like hundreds of her contemporaries. By the early 1940s, MGM studio requested Ball dye her blonde hair red, and she found the hair color to her liking.

Throughout the late 1930s and 1940s, Ball appeared in dozens of movies, dubbing her with the title, "The Queen of B Movies." When Ball appeared in the 1940 film *Dance Girl, Dance,* she met a young, handsome band leader by the name of Desi Arnaz. The two appeared in her next film, *Too Many Girls,* and, by the time filming was over, they were madly in love. November 30, 1940, the couple married in a civil ceremony. The ring given to Ball by Arnaz was from a local drug store since all of the jewelry stores were closed that day. She wore the ring proudly for the rest of their marriage.

While the couple was obviously in love, they spent most of their time apart, with Ball focusing on her film career and Arnaz touring with his Latin orchestra. Friends prophesized that the couple would not last a year, but Ball was madly in love with her new husband's fiery, romantic, Latin style.

In 1944, Ball filed for divorce from Arnaz, citing his many infidelities while touring. The night before the court date, Arnaz met with Ball and asked her to give him one more chance; she agreed and canceled the court date.

Ball continued to focus on her career with the support of Arnaz. The studio was not using Ball in starring roles, and her acting was becoming stagnant. With the urging of Arnaz, Ball appeared in the radio program *My Favorite Husband.* The studio liked what they heard on the radio and decided to cast Ball in a television program of the same format. Ball insisted that she be cast with her real-life husband, but the studio refused to consider Arnaz for the part. Ball refused to do the show, and the husband and wife team went on the road with their new act similar to the radio show that had been so popular. The duo was a huge hit with audiences across the United States, and CBS finally relented, making the *I Love Lucy* show in 1951.

Ball and Arnaz worked with long-time actors William Frawley and Vivian Vance, appearing as the neighbors and landlords to round out the cast. Ball and Arnaz fought the studio to make the show on film, rather than the Kinescope they were using, but the studio refused until Ball and Arnaz agreed to a pay cut to ensure the filming be done to their specifications. Ball and Arnaz created Desilu Production and retained full ownership rights to the show, making the pair one of the first cast to own their programming. The show would be one of the first to use the three-camera set up which became the standard for filming television shows in the future.

On October 15, 1951, *I Love Lucy* hit the airwaves, and audiences loved the new comedy show. A daring break from conventional programming, "Lucy" set the stage for situation comedies for future decades by touching on taboo subjects like working women, marital issues, and childbirth.

The show received five Emmy awards and was nominated twenty times during the run of the show. The program was number one in the ratings for four years running, capturing a 67.3 audience share that had never been done in television history. *I Love Lucy* ran for six years and continues to run in syndication to this day. The cast followed up the success of *I Love Lucy* with *The Lucy-Desi Comedy Hour*, thirteen episodes of which were produced.

While *I Love Lucy* ended in 1957, Desilu productions continued making other top-rated shows like *Our Miss*

Brooks starring Eve Arden, *The Dick Van Dyke Show*, *Star Trek* starring William Shatner, and *Mission Impossible* starring Greg Morris and Peter Graves.

With business and personal friction between the couple growing, Lucy filed for divorce once again in 1960, this time finalizing the split. Ball retained ownership of Desilu Productions, paying Arnaz a handsome sum to keep the business. Arnaz retired to raise horses in Corona, California. Ball remarried to comedian Gary Morton and continued running the studio, the only woman of her generation to run a major television studio. She sold the company to Gulf-Western in 1967 for 17 million dollars, making her the richest woman in show business at that time.

Ball continued her acting career with a follow-up show with Vivian Vance called *The Lucy Show* from 1962 through 1968 and the *Here's Lucy* show from 1968 to 1973. Neither show captured the kind of ratings enjoyed by her first venture, but both enterprises enjoyed modest success. While not the major star she was in the 1950s, Ball was still internationally known and revered by generations of television viewers. Ball had certainly left a permanent mark on the early years of television.

Ball was recognized time and again for her contribution to television. She became the first woman to receive the International Radio and Television Society's Gold Medal. She won four Emmy's® and received the Kennedy Center Honor for Performing Arts for her life's work.

Ball, now semi-retired during the 1970s, attempted to take on a dramatic part in the television movie *Stone*

Pillow which was a modest success. Finally, in 1986, she created a new show, *Life with Lucy*. Unfortunately, the show only aired eight episodes before it was canceled. Ball never worked again in television or film. It was rumored that the canceling of the show caused Ball to fall into a deep depression and Ball's health began to fail as a result. Ball was reclusive for several years towards the end of her life, living in her home in Beverly Hills, California.

In March 1989, Ball appeared on the annual Academy Awards™ broadcast with fellow comedian Bob Hope. The famous duo received a standing ovation from the audience as they entered the stage, a tribute to their legendary status.

On April 18, 1989, Ball complained of chest pain and was rushed to Cedars-Sinai Medical Center, where she was diagnosed with a dissecting aortic aneurysm and underwent heart surgery that lasted for eight hours. Ball was recovering in the hospital four days later when she woke up to severe back pain. The doctors found the aorta ruptured a second time, and Ball fell unconscious. She would never awake as attempts to revive the actress were unsuccessful. Ball died on April 26, 1989, at the age of seventy-seven. Coincidently, the day of Ball's death was the birthday of her long-time friend Carol Burnette, Burnette receiving the flowers sent by Ball just hours after hearing about her friend's death. At CBS studio, the marquee read, "They needed a laugh in Heaven. Goodbye Lucy".

BALL

Henry Durrell Ball
September 25, 1887 - February 28, 1915

Desirée Eveline Hunt Ball
September 21, 1892 - July 20, 1977

Lucille Desirée Ball Morton
August 6, 1911 - April 26, 1989
You've Come Home

A private memorial service for Ball was held at Forest Lawn Memorial park in Hollywood Hills, California. Ball was cremated and interred in the Columbarium of Radiant Dawn at the cemetery. This proved not to be Ball's final resting place, though. In March 2002, Ball's family decided she would be placed in her hometown of Jamestown, New York. The marker on the family plot reads BALL and a large heart with the Ball name in cursive adorns the backside of the monument.

Gracie Allen

The internationally known comedienne, Gracie Allen, loved to play the dim-witted, zany counterpart to her loving straight man husband, George Burns.

Allen was born Grace Ellen Cecile Rosalie Allen on July 26, 1902, in San Francisco, California. The exact year of her birth is a mystery as the records were burned in the great San Francisco fire of 1906. Over the decades, Allen's birth year has been documented as 1895, 1896, 1902, or 1906; take your pick. Burns claimed not to know either, but the year 1902 appears on the front of the crypt where the couple is interred.

Allen appeared for the first time on stage at the age of three with her father, a local entertainer. Allen was encouraged to take dancing lessons by her mother and appeared on stage with her three sisters, billed as "The Four Colleens." After leaving catholic school at the age of fourteen, the girls went on the stage full time. At a very young age, Allen was burned on the arm, which left a terrible scar. Allen wore either long sleeves or three-quarter length sleeves to hide the marks for the rest of her life. Another anomaly was Allen's heterochromia, having one blue and one green eye. While she was very sensitive about her eyes, the abnormality was never mentioned in the act or her personal life.

Allen attempted to leave show business, discouraged by the billing received by her family. She entered secretarial school but never completed the training. By 1922, Allen heard from a friend that the comedy duo of Burns and Lorraine were performing, and Lorraine was leaving the act to find a new partner. Allen went to the theater that evening and mistook Burns for Lorraine. It took three days before Burns admitted to Allen who he really was, but Allen gave the act a chance anyway.

When Allen met Burns, she was betrothed to another man and rejected Burns's marriage proposal on many occasions. Allen finally realized she was in love with Burns when, at a Christmas party in 1925, Burns made her cry, and she said to herself, if he can make me cry, I must be in love. Allen finally accepted Burns's proposal after touring with him for three years, and the two were married on January 7, 1926, and remained married until Allen died in 1964.

Allen performed with her husband on the Vaudeville circuit, finally signing a five-year contract with the Keith Theater chain making Burns and Allen the top-rated act in Vaudeville. The pair continued as the top paid stars on the stage till the late 1930s when friend Eddie Cantor invited Allen to appear on his radio program. The format suited the act perfectly, and Burns and Allen transitioned to radio with relative ease. CBS offered them a contract, and *The Burns and Allen Show* became one of the top three rated shows with an estimated forty-six million listeners each week.

The twosome knew how to work publicity and, in the 1932-33 season, they kept up a yearlong search for Allen's missing brother appearing as a guest on several of the popular radio shows of the 1930s. This gag would have gone further, except Allen's real-life brother asked them to stop since he did not enjoy the gag himself.

In 1940, Allen proclaimed that she would run for the presidency on the Surprise Party ticket. Burns and Allen toured the country by train, appearing on local radio programs on their various stops. The party mascot was a kangaroo, and the motto read, "It's in the Bag." Allen endeared herself to audiences with campaign speeches like, "Everybody knows a woman is better than a man when it comes to introducing bills into the house." and "I don't know much about the Lend-Lease Bill, but if we owe it, we should pay it."

The pair enjoyed consistent success and, in 1948, they decided to give television a try when good friend Jack Benny asked them to join him when he went to work for CBS. *The Burns and Allen show* was a huge success with audiences. It paved the way for many of the successful situation comedies that followed. Allen loved working with her husband but finally retired from the show in 1958 due to health problems. Burns attempted to carry on without her but could not keep the show going without the vivacious Allen by his side.

Allen retired from performing and enjoyed life with her husband and two adopted children. Allen suffered from heart disease, and her health continued to worsen during the years that followed her retirement.

Allen suffered a fatal heart attack on August 27, 1964. Burns was devastated by the loss of his love. In Burns book "Gracie, a Love Story," Burns writes,

The doctor asked Burns if he wanted to see Gracie one last time.

"Of course I did," Burns says. "I wanted to stand next to her onstage and hear the audience laugh. I wanted to hear that birdlike voice. I wanted her to look up at me with her trusting eyes. I wanted to ask her just once more, 'Gracie, how's your brother?'"

For a time, Burns admits:

> *"Things were very, very bad for me. My life was Gracie. But then, about two months later, I started sleeping in her bed— we had twin beds—and things just started turning around for me."*

The funeral service for Allen was held at All Saints Episcopal Church in Beverly Hills, California. A traditional Catholic service was held for the great comedienne, and a private burial followed at the Freedom Mausoleum at Forest Lawn Memorial park in Glendale, California. The obituary notice read:

> *"Comedienne Gracie Allen, half of the comedy team Burns and Allen, died August 27, 1964. She was 59.*
>
> *Allen was born July 26, 1905, in San Francisco, California. The daughter of an entertainer, she made her stage debut at age three as part of her father's song and dance act.*
>
> *Gracie began to be the feature act a few years later. In 1922 she met George Burns, who had recently broken up with his comedy partner William Lorraine.*
>
> *Burns and Allen was soon a comedy duo. Burns played the straight man. The two were a hit. They traveled together for three years before getting married on January 7, 1926, in Cleveland, Ohio.*
>
> *By 1930, Burns and Allen were one of the top vaudeville acts in the United States. In late 1930 CBS signed Burns and Allen to a contract, and within a year, the Burns and Allen*

Comedy Show was one of the most popular radio programs in America.

Allen appeared in several films with her husband during the 1930s, including The Big Broadcast, Six of a Kind, and College Holiday.

When television made its appearance, the Burns and Allen show became an instant hit and continued for eight years from 1950-58. Gracie had tired of her character and wanted to retire.

Allen and her husband lived in Beverly Hills until her death of a heart attack on August 27, 1964."

After Allen's death, Burns visited her monthly, sitting on a marble bench next to her crypt, telling her about anything that was going on in his life at the time. Burns stated that it made him feel better being near her and talking to her. Burns would join his wife on March 9, 1996, thirty-two years later. The crypt front reads Grace Allen and George Burns Together Again, Allen getting top billing.

The Marx Brothers

One of the royal families of comedy, the Marx brothers' name, came to be synonymous with over-the-top slapstick antics with the three oldest siblings dominating Hollywood's golden age with thirty-three feature films and a coast-to-coast stage act.

The Marx family of Germany was known in show business long before the Marx Brothers came to fame. Grandmother Fanny played the harp, and grandfather Levy worked as a ventriloquist. Mother Miene had one brother, Abraham, who later changed his name and became Al Sheen, the comedian.

The Marx family moved to New York when Miene was eighteen years old, and she met Simon Marx. The couple courted for two years before marrying in 1884. The first of the Marx children was born in 1885 but died tragically at seven months. The next of the Marx children born was a son Leonard, born in 1887, followed by Adolf in 1888, Julius Henry in 1890, Milton in 1892, and Herbert in 1901.

The brothers worked odd jobs to support the large family but mother Minnie, as her sons called her, was determined to see her boys be successful in show business

Each of the boys was encouraged to learn a musical instrument. Harpo tried in vain to learn the piano and guitar. When he listened to his grandmother play the harp, he watched intently and taught himself to play. Harpo became an accomplished harpist without ever taking one lesson. Chico took to the piano early, and brother Groucho played the guitar and sang.

As Al Sheen was getting his start in show business, Minnie focused her energy on the boys and their performing career. Chico began playing the piano in pubs while Groucho sang in his high soprano voice as a child. Minnie developed an act for the four older boys called The Four Nightingales. Later Minnie included herself and her aunt Hannah in the act and changed the name to The Six Mascots.

The boys began playing on the Vaudeville stage in 1905 with Groucho as a singing act. By 1907, Gummo joined his brother, and the singing act became a duo. The boys were playing in Texas in 1912 when a horrible noise outside interrupted the act. The audience rushed outside to see what the excitement was, leaving the theater empty while the boys were still on stage. Groucho was infuriated by the interruption and began throwing barbs at the audience when they returned to their seats. The crowd laughed, and the family realized they needed to add comedy to the act.

The brothers then officially changed their names for the act to reflect the nicknames they shared privately. Legend states that the boys got their names during a poker game with Art Fisher. Leonard was called Chico because he enjoyed chasing girls (known as Chickens). Adolf was known as Harpo because of his natural talent for playing the harp. Julius became Groucho because of his temperament for being moody; another story told by Groucho himself is that Groucho was named after a popular comic strip of the day known as Sherlocko the Monk in which there is a character named Groucho the Monk. Milton became Gummo due to his tendency to lurk backstage quietly like a gumshoe cop.

The youngest brother was not named until years later when Gummo left the act; according to several sources, there are three stories to how Zeppo was named.

Harpo claims in his autobiography that Zeppo was named for Zippo, a chimpanzee act they worked with during the Vaudeville years.

In interviews with Chico, he states that he came home one day and found his brother sitting on the fence outside their home. Zeppo greeted him with "Hi Zeke," and Chico responded, "Hi Zeb." The name stuck until years later when the brothers decided Zebbo would not work for the act and change it slightly to Zeppo.

Groucho told a third version of the story during an interview claiming that Zeppo was born during the first flights of the Zeppelins, but this story was discounted later when it was discovered that the Zeppelins did not fly until years after the birth of Zeppo.

The act evolved, and the Marx brother became a hit with audiences as they toured the United States. Brother Gummo decided show business was not to be in his future and joined the armed forces in World War I. Zeppo replaced his brother, and the act continued touring. During this time, the brothers each developed a different character to distinguish each of the four performers. Groucho adopted his trademark greasepaint mustache, cigar, and crouched walk; Harpo became the silent partner due to his inability to keep up with his counterparts' wit with his horn communicating for him on stage his gift of pantomime creating a charm that would be his trademark. Chico honed his accent, becoming the partner to Groucho, and Zeppo became the group's handsome, dapper straight man. The boys satirized anything that happened in their path. High Society, political leaders, and industrial giants were not safe from the barbs of the Marx Brothers.

The brother act was flying high on the Vaudeville circuit, and brother Chico took over managing the group, landing them an offer to appear on Broadway in the musical *I'll Say She Is*. Two more shows followed in the wake of their first success on the stage. *The Cocoanuts* and *Animal Crackers* fit the act perfectly, and The Marx Brothers became a huge success with their slapstick comedy style.

Inevitably, Hollywood came calling for the Marx Brothers, and the act moved to the west coast, signing a contract with Paramount Pictures. The studio capitalized on The Marx Brothers' Broadway fame and adapted the shows *Cocoanuts* and *Animal Crackers* for the big screen starring the brothers in their same roles. Next, the studio cast the boys in the film *The House that Shadow Built* based on their first Broadway show, *I'll Say She Is.*

With each picture, The Marx Brothers' fame grew, but with their next film, *Horse Feathers*, they became superstars and appeared on Time magazine's cover. They continued this success with their next picture, *Duck Soup* which became one of the American Film Institute's top one hundred films of all time. After the release of *Duck Soup,* the Marx Brothers left Paramount due to creative differences. Brothers Zeppo and Gummo gave up performing and worked as successful agents in Hollywood, while Groucho and Chico worked in radio.

MGM executive Irving Thalberg contacted the boys and offered them a contract with his studio. The three remaining Marx Brothers leaped at the offer and began working closely with Thalberg on the next stage of their career.

With Thalberg at the reins, he insisted that the films be more structured and detailed storylines be a fundamental part of the process. He also decided that the team would work out the act on stage before filming to ensure audience reaction. Their next two pictures, *A Night at the Opera* and *A Day at the Races,* were the best films The Marx Brothers had done up to that time. Thalberg died suddenly during the filming of *A Day at the Races,* leaving the boys without an advocate at MGM. Once Thalberg was gone, the brothers found themselves with worsening scripts and left MGM to regain their popularity with another studio. The team continued making pictures until 1933 with RKO Pictures but announced their retirement from the motion picture industry after their film *Lone Happy* in 1949.

During this time, the brother carried on separate family-oriented private lives. Harpo met and married Susan Fleming in 1936, the couple adopted four children, and Harpo became a devoted father. Chico married once in 1917 but divorced his first wife in 1940. He married again in 1958 to Mary De Vithas and stayed with her until his death. Groucho was the ladies' man of the family, married three times from 1920 to 1969, and divorced each woman. Groucho fathered three children with two of his wives. Zeppo married twice and fathered one child with his second wife, Marion Brenda. Gummo married his wife Helen Von Tilzer in 1929, and the couple were together until he died in 1977.

At the end of the 1940s, the brothers went their separate ways, Groucho becoming the Emcee for the wildly popular television show *You Bet Your Life* which ran from 1947 to 1960. Chico created his own big band and toured the country with a teenage Mel Torme as the lead singer of the group.

Throughout the 1950s, the brothers worked together infrequently. They produced a television show called *Deputy Seraph* starring Chico and Harpo, but they finally called off shooting when Chico could not work due to severe arteriosclerosis. All five brothers made only one more appearance together on the television show *Tonight! America After Dark.* This would be the last time The Marx Brothers would be together on screen.

In 1960, writer Billy Wilder presented the team with a new film, *A Day at the U.N.,* but the production was put on hold due to Harpos failing health. The project was abandoned in 1961 after brother Chico died on October 11, 1961, of cardiovascular disease.

At Chico's funeral, the rabbi who stood to give the eulogy had never met the man and knew nothing of what he spoke. It is rumored that Harpo leaned over to his wife and said, "When I go, do me a favor and hire a mime" Chico was interred at the Freedom Mausoleum at Forest Lawn Memorial Park in Glendale, California.

Harpo followed his brother in death in 1964 after suffering from a heart attack and undergoing heart surgery. Years later, Arthur Marx, son of Groucho, said it was the only time in his life he had seen his father cry. Harpo was cremated, and it is rumored but never verified that his remains were scattered in the sand trap on the seventh hole of the Rancho Mirage golf course in California.

Gummo passed away thirteen years later, on April 21, 1977. Older brother Groucho was in such poor health at the time that the family never informed him of his brother's death. Gummo was interred just across the hall from Chico at Forest Lawn Memorial Park in Glendale, California.

Four months later, on August 19, 1977, Groucho died at the age of eighty-six. A private memorial was held at the home of Arthur Marx, Groucho's eldest son. Groucho was cremated, and his remains were interred at Eden Memorial Park in Los Angeles, California.

The last of the Marx Brothers to pass away was Zeppo on November 30, 1979. Following in the footsteps of Harpo, Zeppo was cremated and his remains scattered over the Pacific ocean.

The legacy of the Marx Brothers remains to this day as a testament to the comedic genius of a family that not only worked as a team to great success but as a loving family of supportive, generous, caring men who knew the priority of family above all else.

Bob Hope

Recognized as one of the greatest talents in entertainment history, Bob Hope's name became synonymous with his love of the United States, leaving a lasting legacy of philanthropy and humanitarianism to the soldiers of three wars.

Born Leslie Townes Hope, the fifth of seven sons to a Stone Mason in Eltham, London, England. Hope and his family moved to Cleveland, Ohio, when Hope was five years old, passing through Ellis Island, New York, on their way to a new life in the United States. At the age of seventeen, Hope received his permanent citizenship to the U.S.

Hope began working odd jobs at a very early age to help support the family by dancing and performing comedy. Hope showed promise as an actor at the age of ten by winning a Charlie Chaplin lookalike contest, imitating the comedian perfectly. At the age of fifteen, Hope was admitted into the Boy's Industrial School, known as a reform school for juvenile offenders. In the later years, Hope donated large sums of money to the school.

By 1925, Hope was often performing solo or with partner Lloyd Durbin. Silent Film star Roscoe Arbuckle happened to catch the act one evening and hired the duo to appeared in *Hurley's Jolly Follies*. For the next five years, Hope found great success with several acts of singing, dancing, and comedy. When he met his partner and future wife, Grace Truxell, he attempted to find a career in moving pictures.

In 1930, Hope and Truxell auditioned for famed movie studio Pathe' in Culver City, California. Hope was surprised when the act was turned down. Within a few months, Hope and Truxell divorced, and Hope never spoke of the marriage until a record of the marriage was unearthed years later. In 1934, Hope married Dolores Reade, and the two adopted four children.

Hope tried to have a movie career again in 1934 with Vitaphone pictures in New York starring in a series of twenty-minute film shorts. Hope found modest success with Vitaphone but made a bold career move when he signed a contract with Paramount Pictures in 1938 and moved back to Hollywood, California. It was in the film *The Big Broadcast of 1938* where Hope sang the song *Thanks for the Memories,* which became his theme song for the rest of his life.

The partnership of Hope and Paramount Pictures seemed to produce an endless string of hit movies. Most famous for his "Road" pictures with costar Bing Crosby and Dorothy L'Amour as their love interest, whom they both fought over in every film. Hope became one of Paramount's biggest stars during this time and was considered box office gold in any film production released. Hope enjoyed playing the cowardly man who would seldom get the girl and eventually win against the bad guys despite himself. One of Hope's trademarks on film was breaking the fourth wall to talk to the audience about whatever situation he found himself in. Hope's films always showcased his song and dance style, allowing Hope to introduce many popular songs into American culture.

While Hope held audiences enraptured with his quick wit and impeccable comedic timing in his films, Hope could not seem to gain the approval of the Academy Awards®, which he hosted eighteen times between 1939 to 1977. Hope enjoyed spoofing his desire for the award in several of the "Road" pictures. In *Road to Bali*, Crosby finds Humphrey Bogart's Oscar™ for *African Queen*. Hope grabs is saying, "Give me that; you've got one." Hope, at one memorable Oscar™ ceremony in 1968, during his opening speech, joked, "Welcome to the Academy Awards™, or, as it's known at my house, Passover."

In addition to his movies, Hope appeared on the radio in 1937 with NBC on the *Woodbury Soap Hour*. Hope, once again, enjoyed huge success with radio audiences throughout the 1940s and 1950s on such shows as *The Pepsodent Show, The New Swan Show,* and finally *The Bob Hope Show,* which finally went off the air in 1955.

Hope also collaborated with NBC on several television specials beginning in 1950. Hope appeared on

NBC with several top companies sponsoring the show. Texaco, Chrysler, and General Motors served as the driving force behind the yearly variety shows until 1985. The 1970 and 1971 broadcasts were filmed from Vietnam and became one of the top thirty telecasts in television history, with sixty percent of households watching.

Hope was known for his work entertaining the troops. In 1941, Hope was approached by producer Al Captav to perform at March Air Force Base in California. Hope reluctantly agreed and found the audience reaction nothing short of extraordinary. In 1943, Hope and his troupe of performers traveled to West Africa for the first overseas USO tour. During his lifetime, Hope would do over sixty USO tours over the span of fifty years and four wars. In 1997, an act of congress declared Hope an Honorary Veteran for his years of service to the American troupes.

In 1943, writer John Steinbeck said this about Hope,

"When the time for recognition of service to the nation in wartime comes to be considered, Bob Hope should be high on the list. This man drives himself and is driven. It is impossible to see how he can do so much, can cover so much ground, can work so hard, and can be so effective. He works month after month at a pace that would kill most people."

Hope continued performing well into his nineties. Throughout his career, Hope was honored with every award known. Hope was even given four honorary Academy Awards® for his contribution to film and, in 1960, given the Jean Hersholt Humanitarian Award. In

1985, Hope was presented with a lifetime achievement award by President Ronald Reagan at the Kennedy Center Honors. The following year, Hope was appointed an honorary Knight Commander of the Most Excellent Order of the British Empire by Queen Elizabeth II. All totaled, Hope received over two thousand awards throughout his career.

Hope began suffering from ill-health starting in the year 2000, hospitalized several times over the next three years. Even through these years of poor health, Hope always maintained a sense of humor about himself.

On May 29, 2003, Hope celebrated his one-hundredth birthday. This day was officially known as Bob Hope day in thirty-five states across the United States. Hope celebrated surrounded by family and friends at his home in Toluca Lake, California, where he had lived with his wife Dolores since 1937.

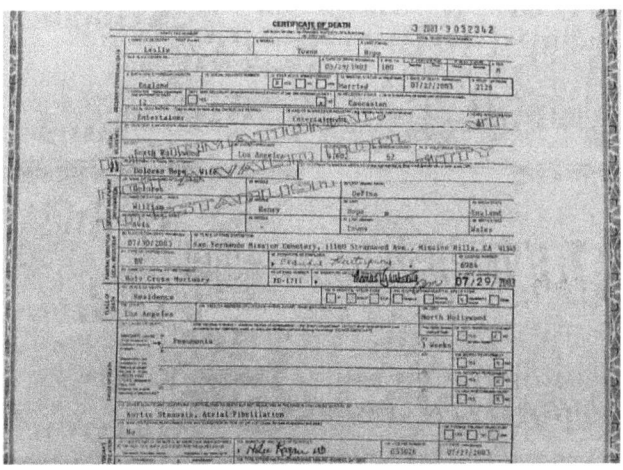

Hope died at his home on July 27, 2003, at the age of one-hundred. Comically enough, Hope was declared dead several times before his actual death. In 1998, Hope's death was announced during a session of congress after the wire service accidentally post an obituary. Once again, in 2003, CNN reported his death after a pre-written obituary was accidentally posted on the internet. Hope took both mistakes in stride. The obituary for Hope was released by NPR:

July 28, 2003 -- *Bob Hope's career stretched from the Jazz Age to the era of the V-chip. He vaulted to the top ranks of vaudeville, dominated the early days of radio, starred on Broadway and moved effortlessly into film and television.*

His wiseguy delivery, fueled by a battery of joke writers on duty around the clock, propelled him to the forefront of show business. His service to American soldiers -- starting with tours of entertainment duty during World War II -- helped make him a national icon.

He died July 27 at the age of 100.

During his heydey, Hope seemed to be everywhere. "Trapped on the treadmill of his own acclaim," was the description provided by the writer John Lahr, who profiled Hope in a New Yorker article. Even in his 90s, Hope made as many as 300 personal appearances a year.

He could sing a little. He could dance a lot. And most of all, he could tell jokes. Giggles and gaggles of jokes, delivered to burlesque-house crowds and the boys on the battleships, from Southern California television studios to U.S.O. stages in North Africa, Korea and Vietnam.

One American generation grew up with Hope and his pal and friendly rival Bing Crosby in the On the Road movies. Another knew him from countless television specials and celebrity golf tournaments on NBC, or as a pitchman for Texaco gasoline and Pepsodent toothpaste…

On July 27, he died at his California home, with his family at his bedside. He outlived many of the people who remembered him at the height of his talents, but the monologue style of comedy he perfected lives on in today's performers. He goes down in history as one of the most celebrated entertainers ever -- a friend of presidents, knighted by Queen Elizabeth, declared an honorary veteran by Congress and holder of more than 50 ceremonial degrees from colleges and universities.

"If I had my life to live over again," Hope once wrote. "I wouldn't have had the strength."

Hope's funeral took place at St. Charles Catholic Church, a few blocks from Hope's home in Toluca Lake. The memorial was a small, private affair, limited to one hundred friends and family members. The Private mass was held at dawn on July 30, 2003. Hope was buried at San Fernando Mission Cemetery, the same cemetery where Hope buried his mother. Years later, San Fernando Mission built the Hope memorial garden, and the entire Hope family was moved to their permanent resting place within the walls of the mission.

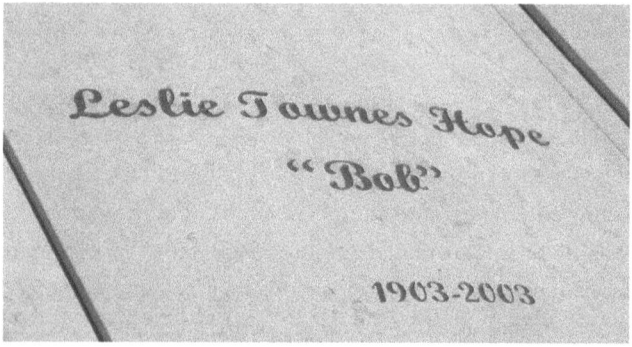

One month after Hope's death, a public memorial was held at St. Charles Catholic Church with many notables attending. Mickey Rooney, Phyllis Diller, Kelsey Grammar, Nancy Reagan, former President Gerald Ford, Sid Caesar, Tom Selleck, Ed McMahon, Barbara Eden, Loni Anderson, Raquel Welch, Shecky Greene, Jack Carter, Connie Stevens, Joey Heatherton, and fellow golfers Jack Nicklaus and Arnold Palmer were just a few of the celebrities who turned out to pay their final respects to the great Bob Hope.

Jack Benny

Recognized as one of the premier entertainers of the twentieth century, Jack Benny mesmerized audiences with his wit, the pregnant pause, and even a sideways glance. Benny's comedy show paved the way for the television situation comedies to come, contemporaries pronouncing Benny, the king of comedy.

Jack Benny was born Benjamin Kubelsky on February 14, 1894, in Chicago, Illinois. The son of immigrant parents, Benny's father, owned a saloon to support his little family. By the age of six, Benny began taking violin lessons, and his parents hoped Benny would become a great classic violinist. By the time Benny entered high school, he had excelled at the instrument but not at his studies. Benny was expelled from school due to his poor grades, failed at trade school, and being an apprentice to his father in his haberdashery.

By the age of seventeen, Benny was performing in Vaudeville and was discovered by Minnie Palmer, the mother of the Marx Brothers. She invited Benny to go on the road with the Marx Brothers act for seven dollars and fifty cents a week. Benny's parents felt their son was too young for this lifestyle and said no to the request.

Shortly after his introduction to the Marx Brothers, Benny met Cora Salisbury, a former Vaudeville performer. Cora was well into middle age and asked Benny to team up with her. The duo billed themselves as *Salisbury and Kubelsky: From Grand Opera to Ragtime* and began performing in 1912. Much to Benny's dismay, another violinist with the same last name of Kubelsky threatened to sue for infringement on the name and notoriety. Benny changed his name to Ben K. Benny, and the act became *Salisbury and Benny*. Within a year, Salisbury retired from show business to care for her mother, and Benny met pianist Lyman Wood. The two men toured together and found much success on the Vaudeville circuit. By 1917, the act was booked into the famous Palace Theater in New York. Success would not be found for the act in New York, and the two men parted ways at the advent of World War II.

Benny enlisted in the United States Navy and began entertaining the troupes with his violin playing and snappy patter routine. During this time, good friend Pat O'Brien told Benny to put down the violin and talk to the audience. Benny found it easy to ad-lib, and his career as a comedian was born.

After leaving the service in 1919, Benny returned to Vaudeville and toured as *Ben K. Benny: Fiddle Funology*.

Once again, Benny found himself involved in a dispute about his name by violinist Ben Bernie and was told to change his name again. Benny tells the story about how the sailors at the time called one another "Jack" instead of fella so he chose the name Jack Benny as his stage name. Benny also dropped the violin playing from the act and billed himself as *Jack Benny: Aristocrat of Humor*.

In 1922, Benny was approached by good friends George Burns and Gracie Allen to develop a new act together. Benny agreed, and the trio enjoyed great success with their new act. One evening after a performance, Benny, Burns, Allen, and Allen's roommate went to dinner, and this was the first time Benny would meet Mary Kelly. The two dated and found romance over the next four years, even with the vigorous touring schedule held by Benny. Legend states that Kelly broke off the relationship with Benny when her father refused to bless the marriage and arranged for her to marry another man. Benny received the news via telegram and was broken-hearted.

Benny continued touring in Vaudeville and found modest success on the stage, eventually earning four hundred and fifty dollars a week, a respectable sum at the time.

Through the years, Benny maintained a close friendship with Zeppo Marx, the youngest of The Marx Brothers. In 1921, Benny was invited to the Marx home for the Passover Seder dinner and was introduced to the Marx daughters Ethel and Sayde. Benny and Sayde Marx took an instant disliking to each other and, by the end of the evening, hated each other according to family legend.

Even with the mutual dislike for each other, fate and time would not allow the two to forget each other.

In 1926, Benny played the Orpheum Theater in Los Angeles, California, and ran into Ethel Marx backstage. Ethel had married fellow Vaudevillian Al Bernovici. Ethel invited Benny to dinner and once again met Sayde. Rumor states that Benny could not take his eyes off the young girl, but, according to Sayde, Benny never looked at her throughout the evening. Either way, Benny was informed that Sayde worked at the May Company department store in the hosiery department and appeared at the store the next day, asking the girl to direct him to the men's room. She continued to be irritated by Benny's constant presence at the store but eventually softened to the man, even attending one of Benny's performances with her steady boyfriend. During the performance, Benny directed several comments to Sayde incensing her beau and resulting in the two leaving before the show's end.

Sayde must have enjoyed the attention, as she agreed to accompany Benny to the Coconut Grove on the last evening he appeared in Los Angeles. Even though they enjoyed each other's company, Benny continued his tour, leaving Sayde behind. It was in 1926 that Benny would run into Sayde's sister Babe Marx in Chicago. Babe informed Benny that Sayde was getting married, and Benny would not hear of it. He called Sayde and told her she was too young to get married and insisted that she come to Chicago to think it over. Once she arrived in Chicago, Benny proposed, and when she asked him why he felt she wasn't too young to marry him, he replied, "To him maybe, but not to me."

Benny and Sayde were married in an Orthodox Jewish ceremony on January 14, 1927, in Waukegan, Illinois. This same year, Benny enlisted his new bride to join him in the act as the dumb girl character of Marie Marsh, following in the footsteps of Burns and Allen. The couple enjoyed enormous success on the east coast and eventually returned to Los Angeles and the Orpheum theater.

By 1928, Benny began a solo career again, working as a master of ceremonies and refining his one-man comedy act. Benny worked steadily, receiving rave reviews in all the major publications of the day. MGM genius Irving Thalberg caught Benny's act and offered Benny a five-year contract with the studio starting at eight hundred and fifty dollars a week.

Benny took the job but found he was dissatisfied with the work offered to him. Benny performed in various two-reel shorts opposite Buster Keaton, Laurel, and Hardy, Lionel Barrymore, and Cliff Edwards, who would later find fame as the voice of Jiminy Cricket for Walt Disney. Within a year, Benny was not offered scripts, but Thalberg refused to release Benny from his contract to work in the theater. Benny was farmed out to rival studios for various projects, much to Benny's disappointment. Finally, in 1929, Thalberg relented and released Benny from his contract to pursue over ventures. Benny and his wife moved back to New York, and Benny took a part in the musical revue *The Vanities,* a bawdy take-off on the Ziegfeld Follies. Benny found massive fame with the show and performed in two hundred and forty-seven shows.

Benny was offered a part in the touring company and turned it down to try his hand in a new arena, radio.

Benny appeared on the radio for the first time on March 29, 1932. Then Broadway columnist Ed Sullivan sponsored the show. Canada Dry executive, N.W. Ayer caught the show, and Benny was offered to host *The Canada Dry Ginger Ale Program* on CBS. By the end of that year, Benny was voted "Most Popular Comedian on the Air" by the listening audience. This was quite an accomplishment for Benny as his competition included the likes of Eddie Cantor, Burns and Allen, Ed Wynn, Al Jolson, and The Marx Brothers, among many others. By 1933, Benny was signed by General Motors for *The Chevrolet Program* on NBC. This show proved short-lived as the president of General Motors, William Knudsen, did not find Benny funny.

Benny remained at the top of his game in radio for the next four years. Benny hired comedy writer Harry Cohn at the beginning of his radio career, and Cohn continued writing for Benny until 1936, when he demanded a salary equal to Benny. Benny refused, and Cohn walked out, leaving Benny without a script for his next show. Benny unceremoniously fired Cohn and hired Sam Perrin and Arthur Phillips with Hugh Wedlock and Howard Snyder to finish the show's last two-week run. Sam Perrin would continue to write for Jack for the next forty years. Benny moved from New York back to Los Angeles, moving his radio show with him to much fanfare on the west coast. Benny brought Sadie Marx to play opposite him in Mary Livingston's role and his butler Eddie "Rochester" Anderson rounding out the cast for

The Jack Benny Show about a penny-pinching performer and his tight-knit group of friends and employees.

Benny was offered movie roles opposite some of the top box office draws of the day. Some of his more popular films include *Washington Slept Here,* co-starring Ann Sheridan, and *The Meanest Man in the World* with Priscilla Lane. Benny appeared opposite Carole Lombard in the film *To Be or Not To Be* in 1942, a role written specifically for Benny. On January 12, 1942, Lombard was killed in a plane crash while on a war bond tour, and the film opened on a sober note on March 6 of that year.

From the 1950s, Benny discovered a trend of families watching more television from their homes rather than going to the theater and agreed to move *The Jack Benny* show to television in 1950. While Mary Livingston enjoyed the radio show, she had developed stage fright over the year and was terrified at the thought of appearing before a live audience each week. She informed Benny she would be leaving the show, and Benny begged her to reconsider. Finally, a compromise was reached, and another actress was hired for the on-screen filming while Mary dubbed the lines from her home after the fact. The audience was none the wiser, and everyone enjoyed the show enormously. The radio show continued to consistent success while the television show continued to grow a large audience. Finally, in 1953, Benny canceled the radio show, although several episodes were rebroadcast from 1956 to 1958. The Jack Benny television show aired from 1950 through 1964 to rave reviews and included guest stars from every arena of show business. Benny won two Emmy Awards®, one in 1957 for Best Male Performance in a series playing himself and another in 1958 for Best Comedy Series.

Benny also appeared on the *GE True Theater* program in 1953. During this time, Benny appeared several times on the show as different characters finding the medium delightful. Benny also appeared on *Shower of Stars* for a total of ten episodes from 1957 to 1958.

It was in 1952 that Benny rediscovered his love for the violin and began practicing in earnest. Benny began playing benefit concerts with the Los Angeles Philharmonic Orchestra and hit the heights of success in 1956, playing a benefit at Carnegie Hall that raised fifty thousand dollars and received one of his best reviews from New York Times critic Harold C. Schonberg. The often misquoted line goes, "Last night at Carnegie Hall, Jack Benny played Mendelssohn. Mendelssohn lost."

Throughout the 1960s and 1970s, Benny continued traveling extensively, raising money for symphonies internationally. Benny appeared annually on *The Jack Benny Christmas Show* and *The Jack Benny Comedy Hour* on NBC. Those closest to Benny could see the star becoming more fragile as the performer hit his 70s and 80s, but he never slowed down and strode out on the stage every evening as the music played with all the energy of a man half his age. In 1974, Benny complained of stomach pain, but friends and family ignored his grumbling due to Benny's propensity for hypochondria. On April 20, 1974, Benny was cast for the movie *The Sunshine Boys* opposite veteran comedian Walter Matthau. The pain worsened in his stomach, but Benny would not give up his touring schedule and continued working on the Christmas special for that year. By December 8, Benny's pain had increased so much that he was prescribed sedatives causing him to cancel an appearance to receive the Louella Parsons Award® from the Hollywood Women's Press Club. Benny asked good friend George Burns to stand in for him at the ceremony. Benny also asked Burns to take over the role in *The Sunshine Boys*. Just days later, on December 20, Benny was diagnosed with pancreatic cancer.

Doctors continued to sedate Benny as he rested quietly in his home. On December 25, Benny's press agent released a statement that caused a worldwide stir of concern and sympathy. The next day, Benny died quietly, surrounded by friends and family.

Jack Benny's funeral was held on December 29, 1974, at Hillside Memorial Park in Culver City, California. Over one thousand people attended the event as Comedian Bob Hope delivered a tearful eulogy, and George Burns spoke only these words, *"What can I tell you about Jack?" he began, "I can't imagine life without him."*

Burns broke down while attempting to memorialize his friend and had to be helped to his seat. Also in attendance were fellow comedians Groucho Marx, George Jessel, Jack Lemmon, and Milton Berle. After the emotional service, Pallbearers Gregory Peck, Frank Sinatra, and Milton Berle carried Benny to his final resting place in a black marble crypt marked by the epitaph "A Gentle Man."

Unknown to even those closest to Benny is the story that Benny sent flowers to his beloved wife regularly. On one occasion, Benny informed the florist, "If anything should happen to me, I want you to send my doll a red rose every day." Benny's request was honored, and a rose arrived every day at the Benny home until June 30, 1983, when Benny's wife passed away and was laid to rest with her beloved husband.

Edgar Bergen

Along with his wooden sidekicks Charlie McCarthy and Mortimer Sneard, Ventriloquist Edgar Bergen created a world of entertainment with his inanimate friends, making them as real to the audience as any flesh and blood performer.

Edgar Bergen was born Edgar Berggren on February 16, 1903, in Chicago, Illinois, to Swedish immigrant parents. The Bergen family moved to Decatur, Michigan, while Bergen was still a small boy. At the age of eleven, Bergen sent away for a booklet on Ventriloquism. Within a few years, Bergen had perfected his skills at the art and commissioned his first dummy Charlie McCarthy by the age of sixteen. The puppet's original name was Charlie Mack, named after the wood smith that fashioned the creation for Bergen. The likeness of the puppet is rumored to be the likeness of a newspaper boy who was a precocious youngster Bergen knew.

Bergen began performing in Vaudeville theaters and silent movie houses to earn a living while going to school in Chicago. Bergen earned enough money to pay his tuition to Northwestern University while working on the stage.

After school, Bergen changed his name permanently and moved to New York. While working at a party one evening, Bergen was discovered by gossip columnist Elsa Maxwell and was offered a job at the famous Rainbow Room. During his tenure at the club, Bergen was seen by the elite of New York society as well as producers from some of the best-known radio programs of the day. Bergen was offered a guest spot on the *Rudy Valle Show* in 1936 and was a hit with audiences. The smart patter of Bergen and his partner enchanted listeners who felt like the puppet had real conversations with his human partner.

The following year, Bergen was offered his own show, and the initial broadcast went on the air on May 9, 1937. The show ran until 1956, with Bergen reaching the heights of stardom with his little wooden accomplice. As the show progressed, Bergen introduced other characters like the slow-witted Mortimer Sneard and the manhunter Effie Klinker. While the audience enjoyed the variety of characters, Charlie McCarthy was the star with his childlike voice and smart-aleck wisecracks. While on radio, the listeners could not see that Bergen had a tendency to move his lips, but Charlie McCarthy would refer to Bergen's lack of skill, which became an integral part of the act.

In 1941 while performing on the radio before a live audience, Bergen caught a glimpse of a young woman in the front row and enjoyed looking at the slender woman throughout the broadcast. After the show, Bergen requested to meet the woman. He was introduced to Frances Westerman, a fashion model. Bergen was twenty years her senior, but the two began dating and, within one year, they married in Mexico. On May 9, 1946, Frances gave birth to their first child, Candice Bergen, who later had a very successful film and television career.

While Bergen enjoyed enormous success on radio, he segwayed into motion pictures and worked with some of the top box office stars of the day. The duo appeared in the 1938 film *The Goldwyn Follies* starring dance team the Ritz Brothers and followed up with *You Can't Cheat an Honest Man* working opposite megastar W.C. Fields. In 1938, Bergen was given an honorary Academy Award® for his creation of Charlie McCarthy. Bergen continued success in film throughout the 1940s and, by 1950, transitioned once again to the new medium of television.

While Bergen was never offered his own show on television, he did appear on numerous well-known shows like *What's My line* and *Do You Trust Your Wife?* Bergen found approval in whatever entertainment field he chose, along with his cast of characters working with. For five decades, every star in Hollywood wanted to work with this great performer until he finally retired from entertaining in 1978 at the age of seventy-five. Bergen announced in mid-September that he would be leaving show business and marked the occasion with a two-week engagement at Cesar's Palace in Las Vegas, Nevada. Three days after his final performance, on September 30, 1978, Bergen died in his sleep due to kidney disease.

During the course of his career, Bergen had three versions of Charlie McCarthy created. Upon his death, the original puppet was given to the Smithsonian Institute in Washington D.C., the second resides at the Museum of Broadcast Communications in Chicago, Illinois, and the third was purchase by magician David Copperfield for his private collection.

At the funeral of Bergen, Jim Henson stood with his famed puppet Kermit the Frog, and Kermit gave a beautiful eulogy for the great performer. After the private service, Bergen was buried at Inglewood Memorial Park in Los Angeles, California, under a large family stone.

Jimmy Durante

The universal performer known as Jimmy Durante was equally known as an actor, comedian, songwriter, singer, and composer. Best recognized by his large nose and gravel tone voice which made him one of the best-known personalities from the 1920s through the 1970s.

Jimmy Durante was born the third of four children to an Italian-American family in New York City on February 10, 1893. Durante's father, a barber, found his bride through a mail order bride service and married Rosa, after which they settled in Brooklyn, New York.

Durante took to the piano at an early age and enjoyed playing ragtime and jazz, rather than the classical music that was more socially acceptable at the time. Durante did not enjoy school and dropped out in the eighth grade to pursue a career in music, playing the piano full time with his cousin, who was also named Jimmy Durante. The duo did not last as Durante found his cousin unprofessional and undisciplined. Durante became a solo act, playing the piano bars of New York under the name "Ragtime Jimmy." At the beginning of the 1920s, Durante joined the "Original New Orleans Jazz Band" and found fame with the group as the comic relief during the shows. Within a short time, the band name was changed to "The Jimmy Durante's Jazz Band."

By the mid-1920s, Durante left the band and went on the road with his two best friends Lou Clayton and Eddie Jackson. The three men enjoyed modest success together, writing songs, singing, and doing their comedy act. Durante continued touring for the next ten years to modest success on the stage.

By 1934, Durante was touring and wrote a cute little tune titled *Inka Dinka Doo*. Unbeknownst to him, this became his theme song for the rest of his career. Durante began performing on Broadway in hit shows like *Jumbo, Show Girl,* and *Strike me Pink*. Durante also appeared on the radio as a guest star on several popular programs with celebrities like Eddie Cantor, Gary Moore, and Frank Sinatra. After Cantor left *The Chase Sanborn Hour,* Durante took over for him as host of the popular radio show. By the next year, Durante hosted his own show, *The Jumbo Chief Fire Program,* sponsored by Texaco. Durante signed off each show with the line "*Good night, Mrs. Calabash, wherever you are.*" Throughout his life, interviewers asked Durante who the mysterious Mrs. Calabash was, but he never gave up the mystery. Many years later, there were several stories as to the secret to the strange reference. One story goes that the band stopped in Calabash, North Carolina, at a restaurant for dinner. He so enjoyed the food and atmosphere that he promised the owner he would make her famous. While not knowing the woman's name, Durante referred to her as Mrs. Calabash every evening. Another theory was that Durante was referring to his first wife, Jeanne Olsen, who died on Valentine's Day in 1943 after twenty-two years of marriage. Finally, in 1966, Durante revealed in an interview with the National Press Club Meeting that it was a pet name for his wife, whom he adored.

While Durante found fame in Vaudeville, radio, and on Broadway, a new calling drew him to the west coast as Durante tried his hand at motion pictures. Durante began getting his feet wet in moving pictures with the silent film *The Wet Parade* starring Buster Keaton in 1932, followed by *Broadway to Hollywood* in 1933. Durante only appeared in a handful of pictures throughout his career, but his memorable songs and snappy patter made each film unforgettable. His final film appearance was in the 1963 classic. *It's a Mad Mad Mad Mad World* literally kicking the bucket in the film after revealing the location of buried treasure to a group of money-hungry scavengers.

The 1960s brought many changes to the life of Durante. In 1961, Durante married a second time, and the couple adopted a daughter, Cecilia Anne. Durante did voice-over work for the classic Christmas feature *Frosty the Snowman* for Rankin & Bass, which became a timeless television classic. Kellogg's hired Durante as a spokesman for their Corn Flakes breakfast cereal, introducing him to a whole new generation of fans.

Durante continued to be bigger than life to fans throughout five decades of performances. Even after Durante suffered a stroke and was bound to a wheelchair in 1972, he was immortalized in film and television with character after character making impressions of Durante made him famous during his career. Durante's famous "Everybody wants ta get inta the act!" and "Ha-cha-cha-chaaaaaaa!" was used in countless cartoons and films.

After retiring from show business after his stroke, Durante spent the next eight years living quietly with his wife in Santa Monica, California. Durante suffered several more strokes, causing his health to deteriorate significantly. On January 29, 1980, Jimmy Durante died of pneumonia at Saint John's Hospital in Los Angeles, California.

The funeral of Durante was held at Good Shepherd Catholic Church in Beverly Hills, California. After a private funeral mass, Durante was buried at Holy Cross Cemetery in Culver City, California, under a simple stone that reads "Beloved Husband and Father."

Jackie Gleason

The infamous Jackie Gleason was born to a poor Irish Catholic family in Brooklyn, New York, on February 26, 1916. His given name Herbert John, but he was nicknamed Jackie. Living with his mother, Mae, and his father John, an insurance clerk, Gleason's parents scraped by on a meager twenty-five dollars a week, which caused turmoil in the family. Mae felt that her husband owed her the finer things in life, accusing her husband of not providing properly for the family. John resented his wife and her constant demands. The couple both drank heavily, causing them to erupt into fights that terrified young Gleason. The death of Gleason's younger brother due to Nephritis when Gleason was only three caused additional chaos increasing the dissention between his parents. By the time Gleason was eight years old, his father had left Mae and her young son. Mae worked as a subway token agent to feed her small family, but they constantly struggled for money.

Gleason attended John Adams High School in Queens, New York but dropped out before graduation. He joined a street gang and spent his days learning to play pool and hanging around the local athletic club where he learned to box and play football. By the time Gleason was nineteen, his mother had died, and he was sent to live with his grandmother.

Gleason had a sharp wit about himself, enabling him to enter a local talent contest with his self-written comedy routine. Shortly after winning the contest, Gleason found himself as the Master of Ceremonies for the Folly Theater in Brooklyn. Gleason worked as a carnival barker, comic, and emcee traveling around New York to find work wherever he was needed.

In 1935, Gleason worked as a D.J at station WAAT in Newark, New Jersey, and married his high school sweetheart, Genevieve Halford, the following year.

By then, Gleason received great reviews and became a popular comic in New York and New Jersey. Gleason expanded to Philadelphia and Long Island, growing his popularity. Finally, Broadway came calling, and Gleason took part in the show *Along Fifth Avenue* to decent reviews. Producer Jack Warner attended the show one night and found Gleason's comedic acting amusing. Warner offered the young man a movie contract, and Gleason agreed immediately. He moved to Hollywood while leaving his wife and two daughters back in New York. Gleason struggled at first, performing in several less than memorable films while performing in Los Angeles comedy clubs at night. Gleason gave up on Hollywood and moved back to New York, appearing on Broadway in *Follow the Girls*. Gleason was a hit, and, following the close of the show, he appeared in the fashionable supper clubs in Manhattan with his stand-up comedy act.

The year was 1949, and television was becoming more popular with families across the United States. Gleason was offered a role in the television show *The Life of Riley*, one of the first family situation comedies. The show had been a long-running radio program starring William Bendix, but producer Irving Brecher decided to adapt the show for television, offering Gleason the starring role. Gleason enjoyed a successful season, but the program only ran from October 1949 to March 1950. Gleason found himself unemployed once again and appeared on *Dumont's Cavalcade of Stars*, a long-running television show hosted by Jerry Lester. When Lester left the show, Gleason stepped in as master of ceremonies creating several characters, but the most beloved was Ralph Kramden, a boisterous, Bus Driver from New York with a propensity for get rich quick schemes.

Gleason created a major stir for CBS and was offered a contract to do his own show. Gleason took the offer, and production began on *The Jackie Gleason Show* in 1951, a variety sketch show. Gleason continued his Ralph Kramden character with a six-minute sketch each week. Ratings for the show soared, dubbing Gleason "Mr. Saturday Night." By 1955, Gleason was so popular CBS decided to split the show and make it two half-hour programs, one situation comedy, and one variety show. With that, *The Honeymooners* was born. Costarring Art

Carney, Audrey Meadows, and Joyce Randolph, *The Honeymooners* showcased the foursome as working-class men with the battleax wives always looking for a break. Carney played the scatter-brained Norton, the best friend that always managed to bungle any plan. The thirty-nine original shows are considered classics of television history, but Gleason left the show behind in 1956 when ratings began to drop, and they were running out of original ideas.

By then, Gleason was making ten thousand dollars per week, and his extravagant lifestyle caused him to burn through the money as quickly as it came in. Gleason purchased several large mansions in upstate New York, expensive suits, automobiles, and threw lavish parties with thousands of dollars of liquor.

During the 1950s & 1960s, Gleason recorded several popular record albums highlighting popular music and wrote music for his television shows. In 1961, Gleason gave the motion picture industry another try with the part of Minnesota Fats in the motion picture *The Hustler,* which garnered him an Academy Award® nomination for Best Supporting Actor®. That same year, Gleason wrote, produced, and starred in the film *Gigot*, a notorious box office flop. Throughout the 1960s, Gleason appeared in one bad movie after another and was denied the role of Popeye Doyle in *The French Connection*, a rolewhich he desperately wanted to play. Gleason once again abandoned movies. It was not until 1977 that he was seen on screen again as the comical Buford T. Justice in the box office blockbuster *Smokey and the Bandit* costarring Burt Reynolds and Sally Fields. Gleason reprised his role in

1980 and again in 1983 for two sequels to the franchise. Gleason's final film role was in the 1986 comedy-drama *Nothing in Common* starring Tom Hanks. Gleason playing the role of Hanks aging father, whom Hanks is forced to take care of after the end of his parent's marriage. The film was not considered a box office or critical success, but the film gained popularity with Hanks's rise to fame in later years.

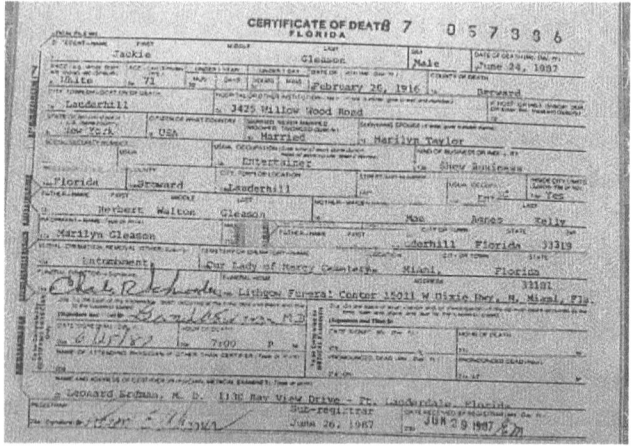

In 1978, Gleason underwent triple bypass surgery to repair severe blockage in his heart. His health never fully recovered, but Gleason continued working periodically. Gleason also suffered from colon and liver cancer in the last years of his life. Although his health was in demise, Gleason continued smoking five packs of cigarettes a day and drinking heavily. On June 24, 1987, he passed away at the age of 71 in Fort Lauderdale, Florida.

A private funeral mass was held for the family at the Cathedral of St. Mary in Miami, Florida. Gleason was laid to rest at Our Lady of Mercy Catholic Cemetery in a large private outdoor mausoleum. On the base of the steps, read the infamous line "And Away We Go."

The Three Stooges

Known as one of the greatest slapstick comedy teams in the history of film, The Three Stooges were comprised not of three but five different comedic performers over the years plus a sixth straight man. The combination proved to be the perfect recipe for physical comedy and quick wit in the traditional burlesque style, making the Three Stooges a timeless American icon.

A family of five brothers born in Bensonhurst a small Jewish community in New York. Shemp, the oldest of the Horowitz brothers, was born on March 17, 1895, brother Moe followed on June 19, 1897, and the baby Jerome, later known as Curly, was born on October 22, 1903. There were two younger brothers in the family, but they were unknown, going into other lines of work and stayed out of the show business spotlight.

The oldest, Shemp, was born Samuel Horowitz, but the nickname came from his grandmother, who could not pronounce his name properly. The rest of the Horowitz family adopted the name, and Shemp was born. A mischievous child, Shemp enjoyed flushing everything from books to sweaters down the family toilet. Shemp even took his brother Irving's history book apart page by page, which garnered a head slap from his mother, a slap with a belt from his father, a kick in the pants from Moe, and a shove from Irving.

Shemp finished school at PS 163 in Brooklyn, New York, and attended New Utrecht High School. He did not finish his senior high education but agreed to attend a trade school, practicing to be a plumber. As a teenager, Shemp left his mischievous ways behind him and became a very serious young man. He showed no interest in going into show business but was eventually coerced by Moe to join his act with straight-man Ted Healy.

The second oldest, Moe, was the first to enter show business. Throughout his school years, Moe had a head of luxurious curly hair that he was taunted about for years by his schoolmates. Moe's mother, always wanting a girl, enjoyed dressing Moe's hair and kept it long. Unable to stand the teasing anymore, Moe took a pair of shears and chopped off the locks until what was left resembled the signature haircut he would sport for the rest of his life.

An avid reader, Moe had an affinity to memorize most anything and read his brother Jack's books. Horatio Alger was Moe's favorite writer, and it was said that these novels gave Moe many of his ideas for the act later in life. Although Moe excelled at school, he did not have any interest in learning and would play hooky to go to the local theaters to ask any passerby to purchase him a ticket for the show since juveniles could not obtain tickets for themselves. Moe would sit in the balcony and watch the entire performance, focusing his attention on one specific actor each time he attended to study each facet of the routine.

Moe's marks in school reflected his missing days, but he still completed his education through primary school at P.S. 163 in Brooklyn, New York. Moe attended high school for only two months before dropping out completely to go into show business. His parents pled with him to attend a trade school, and he agreed, enrolling in Baron DeHirsch Trade School in New York as an electrician. Although he put his best effort into his learning a trade, Moe left the school after only a few months, longing for his first love, the theater.

The youngest of the three brothers was Jerome. As a small child, Curly was quiet and reserved. The two older siblings enjoyed playing with their youngest brothers, putting him in his modified soapbox racer baby carriage and wheeling the infant all over town.

Curly got his first taste of show business at the age of four, being cast in one of his brother's basement productions. The kids charged the neighborhood children two cents to come watch the plays, and Curly enjoyed making people laugh.

Curly struggled throughout his school years and eventually dropped out. He adored his older brothers and followed them where ever they went. Moe took his young brother to the local Vaudeville houses and theaters, where Curly learned to love comedy and musicals.

Curly enjoyed dancing and became an accomplished ballroom dancer. He was admired for his beautiful singing voice and was in demand for social events throughout the neighborhood.

Moe got his first taste of filmmaking in 1909 when he became an errand boy at Vitagraph Studio in New York. He worked hard and did not accept tips from the performers. This earned Moe the respect of several top box office stars of the day, and soon Moe found himself appearing as a bit player in films starring Flora Finch, John Bunny, and Walter Johnson.

This same year, Moe met the man who became his lifelong friend, Ted Healy. The two young men became fast friends and joined forces that summer traveling with the Annette Kellerman aquatic act of diving girls. The job only lasted one summer, and the two men parted ways to go on with their solo careers. It would not be until 1922 when they met again.

Moe and brother Shemp developed a new Vaudeville act, trying their hand at singing in local taverns and performing in black face on the stage for the next few years.

In 1922, Ted Healy contacted Moe, asking him to join Healy on the road. Moe and Shemp answered the call, and the trio toured Vaudeville, polishing their comedic skills. Curly enjoyed following them, supporting his brother's success by bringing them sandwiches between performances and watching from backstage as they performed their slapstick comedy.

In 1925, Moe met and married Helen Schonberger, cousin to the great Harry Houdini. Within a few weeks of becoming Mrs. Moe Howard, Helen begged Moe to leave show business and stay by her side as she was expecting a child. Moe agreed and attempted a career in real estate for a year. Moe noticed he did not have a mind for selling property, Moe opened a retail store and lost everything but the shirt on his back. Finally, Moe went back to the theater, producing and directing plays in the small town where he and his bride lived. This proved an utter failure also as Moe had no sense for staging plays. Finally, Moe accepted his limitations at real-world work and went back to performing with his group of long-time friends, touring with *A Night in Venice*, a successful Vaudeville troupe.

That same year, the group met a young struggling comic performer by the name of Larry Fine. Fine, with his frizzy hair and pinched voice, became a welcome addition to the act.

Born Louis Fienberg in Philadelphia, Pennsylvania, Fine grew up in a middle-class home to parents who owned a jewelry and watch repair shop. As a young boy, Fine was badly burned on the arm as a result of playing with acid used at the shop to test metals for gold. Fine went through painful skin grafts, and the doctors recommended to his parents that Fine should learn to play the violin as a therapy to repair the damaged muscles. Fine became so proficient at playing that he started performing locally and winning amateur contests.

Fine enjoyed entertaining as a child, and this thirst developed during his teen years. Fine performed for anyone who would watch. He expanded his musical knowledge, included other instruments like saxophone, clarinet, and piano. Besides his love for music, Fine became a boxer and fought in over forty bouts during his short career.

In 1921, Fine joined Gus Edward's Newsboy Sextet playing the violin and telling jokes. It was here that he met his future wife, Mabel. Mabel and her sister joined Fine, and they called the act *The Haney Sisters and Fine*. They toured together until 1925, when Ted Healy approached Fine to become a Stooge.

The act toured to great triumph until 1930, when they were invited to perform in their first feature-length film for Twentieth Century Fox.

When Healy decided to leave the show and take the brothers with him to Hollywood, the brothers agreed and moved to the west coast to find work in motion pictures. With their following on the stage and Healy working as their agent, they found work almost immediately after arriving in Los Angeles.

Their first film, *Soup to Nuts,* found the group playing firemen with Moe being billed as Harry Howard in the credits. Shemp received the lion's share of the lines in the movie, and people assumed he was the leader. The film was a success and was followed by a series of comedy shorts featuring Moe, Larry, and Curly, with straight man Healy rounding out the team. Shemp left Hollywood after their first film and returned to the east coast stage in a solo act. The team performed in many successful short featurettes during this time, and the Three Stooges became very popular with audiences.

In 1934, Healy decided to move forward with a solo career, signing a contract with Metro Goldwyn Mayer while the trio signed with Columbia Pictures to a very lucrative contract. It is rumored that the boys started making six hundred dollars each per picture, although others say it was closer to one thousand dollars. They signed a one-year contract with producer Harry Cohn with the option to renew. Cohn saw the incredible draw of the trio at the box office but purposefully made sure the boys never knew their true value to the studio. For the next twenty-three years, the Stooges worked for Cohn, never once asking for or being offered a raise in salary.

The only loophole in the contract was the thirteen weeks the boys were allowed to tour the country doing personal appearances, which greatly increased their income.

The act consistently worked as the childlike antics charmed audiences and the physically taxing slapstick comedy of hair-pulling, eye-gouging, and face-slapping. The bald, chubby Curly became the most popular of the Three Stooges, although he was fiercely insecure about his acting abilities. An introvert off the set, Curly rarely spoke to anyone, the complete antithesis of his on-screen character. To calm his nerves, Curly ate, drank, and enjoyed the company of women to excess, which caused his health to deteriorate as his weight ballooned to over three hundred pounds. On January 23, 1945, he entered the Cottage Hospital in Santa Barbara, California, where he was diagnosed with extreme hypertension, a retinal hemorrhage, and obesity.

On May 6, 1946, Curly suffered a stroke while filming *Half-Wits Holiday*. He took a leave of absence, thinking he would return to work, but suffered another severe stroke in 1949, which ended his career forever.

Curly was admitted into the Motion Picture Country House and Hospital on August 29, 1950, and lived out the rest of his life in and out of nursing homes until his death on January 18, 1952, at the age of forty-eight. A traditional Jewish funeral was performed, and Curly was laid to rest at Home of Peace Memorial Park in Los Angeles, California. His upright headstone reads Beloved Husband, Father, and Brother with a traditional Jewish star etched into the headstone.

After his death, fans would visit the grave and leave small stones as tokens to remember the life of this once great comedian. Over the years, the fans have spelled out the Nyuk Nyuk Nyuk, the laugh that became Curly's trademark during his life.

It was after Curly's first stroke that Moe approached Shemp to join the group once again. Shemp agreed hesitantly, having a very fruitful career of his own. He finally accepted, knowing his brothers would be left in the cold without the Three Stooges act. Shemp fell back into his Stooge role easily and appeared in seventy-six more short subjects to great success. During this time, Fine was given more screen time, offering him an opportunity to show audiences that he was more than a background character to break up the fights.

In 1952, Columbia Pictures began phasing out the short subject films and fired producer Hugh McCollum causing director Edward Bends to leave the studio out of loyalty to his friend. This left the Stooges with director Jules White, who felt they could cut production costs further by recycling old film footage and filming a minimum of new scenes with the boys. At first, the productions value maintained good quality but quickly deteriorated to meager value films with most of the footage used from previous pictures.

By 1955, the boys were working infrequently at the studio, and by the end of that year, Shemp died suddenly of a heart attack, leaving Moe and Fine to finished the final four pictures without the third Stooge. The studio worked around Shemp, using his old films to fill in the gaps, but the boys knew they would need a replacement quickly. The death of Shemp came as a shock as the man was returning from a boxing match with friend Al Winston. They were sharing a taxi when Shemp, in the middle of a joke, suddenly slumped over and died of a massive heart attack on November 22, 1955. A small private funeral was held for the family, and Shemp was interred in a crypt at Home of Peace Memorial Park, just steps away from his brother.

The following year, comedian Joe Besser was offered the third position, and he accepted the role. Besser was enamored with show business, primarily magic and stage performing. Besser spent most of his days at the Vaudeville theater instead of attending school, but his parents encouraged his love of performing. Even as a child, Besser worked to pass out handbills for the local theater and also work for Western Union. Desperate to become a magician, Besser approached renowned magician Howard Thurston asking to join his act. For five years, Thurston rejected Besser, who told him to wait till he was older. Finally, in 1920, Besser stowed away on the train the night Thurston's show closed, and Thurston found him sleeping among the props the next morning when the train pulled into Detroit station. Besser became the comic relief, seemly to foil Thurston's magic feats by letting the audience in on the gag.

By 1923, Besser found his love of comedy and began touring the Vaudeville circuit along with Sam Critcherson. Finally, Besser became a headliner on the Orpheum circuit, eventually making his way to the Broadway stage in New York.

In 1938, Besser was approached by producer Irving Briskin and offered a contract with Columbia Pictures. By the mid-1940s, Besser was a well-known comedian in Hollywood, being offered guest spots on *The Jack Benny Show*, *The Fred Allen Show,* and *Tonight on Broadway*. Throughout the 1940s and the first part of the 1950s, Besser maintained continued success on television and in feature film shorts for Columbia.

In 1956, Besser began performing with The Three Stooges and enjoyed his time with Moe Howard and Larry Fine. In an interview, Besser was quoted as saying,

"Moe and Larry were great. We had a lot of fun, and I had no problems with them. I knew them when they were with Ted Healy. So, we all went back some years together. After the Healy days, I continued to follow their careers. I'm glad I did join the Stooges, and I have never regretted it."

Besser only performed in a total of sixteen short films before the studio closed down production on The Three Stooges. Moe and Larry starting to show their age, and the physical comedy became more labored. The studios did not maintain a budget for the short films, and finally, in December 1957, Columbia ended their association with The Three Stooges.

The boys attempted to stay together, doing personal appearances, but Besser finally opted out of the act in 1959 due to his wife's failing health. This looked like the end of The Three Stooges.

During this time, television had created a new market for the short subject films of the Three Stooges. The television stations purchased these old films, and a new generation of Stooges fans was born. Moe and Larry quickly hired burlesque comic Joe De Rita as the third Stooge. The trio made several full-length feature films from 1959 to 1965, appealing to the kid matinee market of the era. *Have Rocket, Will Travel, The Three Stooges Met Hercules,* and *Snow White, and the Three Stooges* were some of the more popular films by the group.

In addition to their film career, the Three Stooges became the most popular live act in America, traveling the country throughout the 1960s. The Stooges also created an animated series that consists of One hundred fifty-six animated shorts produced for television.

At the end of 1969, the Stooges went into production of a live-action television series, but Fine suffered a near-fatal stroke during the filming of the pilot episode ending his career and the show. Over the next four years, Fine suffered several more strokes, eventually dying on January 24, 1975, at the age of seventy-two. The funeral of Fine was held at the Church of the Recessional at Forest Lawn Memorial Park in Glendale, California. The small service was concluded, and Fine was interred in the Freedom Mausoleum next to his wife with a simple marker with his name and birth and death year.

Fine is interred near comedy greats Chico and Gummo Marx of The Marx Brothers fame.

Moe was devastated by his friend's death but soon followed, succumbing to lung cancer on May 4, 1975, at the age of seventy-seven. Moe's funeral was held at Hillside Memorial Park chapel in Culver City, California, after which he was interred in an outdoor mausoleum in the cemetery.

Besser followed in death on March 1, 1988, succumbing to heart failure. Joe De Rita, the last surviving member of the Three Stooges, passed away on July 3, 1993, after suffering several strokes. De Rita was interred at Valhalla Memorial Park in Los Angeles; the epitaph on his simple headstone reads "The Last Stooge."

Danny Kaye

Danny Kaye was born David Daniel Kaminsky on January 18, 1913, in Brooklyn, New York, to Jewish-Ukrainian immigrant parents. Kaye was the youngest of the three sons, Kaye being the only child born in the United States; his brothers both were born in Ekaterinoslav.

Kaye found he could entertain his friends at school with his funny personality and singing voice. Kaye continued to grow as a comedian with his mother's support, who died when Kaye was a young teenager. A poor student, Kaye dropped out of school soon after her death at the age of thirteen and ran away from home with his best friend Louis, settling in Florida to become a "busker" singing on the streets for money. Finding no luck advancing his career on the streets, Kaye moved back to New York and took a series of odd jobs, including office clerk, a soda jerk, insurance adjuster, and dental technician. Kaye was fired from each job and finally gave up on working in society.

Kaye changed his name and moved to the Catskills in New York to work for the hotels and camps performing comedy and singing. Finding modest success, Kaye joined the dance team of Dave Harvey and Kathleen Young. The trio toured and found great success on the east coast. By 1933, the team worked steadily, but Kaye wanted more from his life than the meager fame that came with performing in nightclubs.

In 1934, Kaye traveled to the Orient and learned singing, dancing, mime, and performance skills. During his tour, a typhoon hit the hotel where he stayed, and Kaye was almost killed when a large structure hit his room. Kaye learned the art of pantomime during his stay in Japan, entertaining an audience that did not speak English.

The next year, Kaye performed his debut in London to poor reviews. In 1938, Kaye came back to the United States and met writer Sylvia Fine in the Poconos mountains of New York. Fine's comedy style was well suited to Kaye, and the team wrote several of Kaye's more famous routines like "Pavlova" and " Stravinsky." Kaye and Fine soon became more than a writing team falling in love and finally becoming husband and wife on January 3, 1940.

Cshow *Straw Hat Revue*. Kaye became a sensation with his tongue twister way of speaking along with his song and dance routines. By 1940, Kaye performed in nightclubs, on Broadway, and touring with the USO to entertain the troops during World War II.

It was in 1943 that Samuel Goldwyn discovered Kaye and offered him a contract with MGM Studios. Kaye was featured in the 1943 film *Up in Arms* starring Dana Andrews and singing sensation Dinah Shore. Kaye had appeared in several short subject films before his feature film debut, but his performances in these films were forgettable at best.

In addition to film, Kaye was offered his own radio show, *The Danny Kaye Show,* on CBS. This show only lasted one year, ending in 1946. Kaye asked to be released from the contract when the show did not take off, and audiences stopped tuning in. The show organizers agreed, and Kaye went on to focus his talents on the big screen.

By the beginning of the 1950s, Kaye was a household name performing in many notable roles, but the best was yet to come for Kaye. In 1952, Kaye portrayed children's writer Hans Christian Anderson in the film of the same name. By 1954, Kaye was cast in *White Christmas*; the film was originally written for Fred Astaire and Donald O'Connor. Kaye played opposite veteran actor/singer Bing Crosby in the light-hearted musical comedy, which also starred Rosemary Clooney and dancer Vera Ellen. With the film's success, Kaye was offered the starring role in *The Court Jester* opposite Basil Rathbone and an unknown John Carradine. His performance in the film is considered by most to be Kaye's best work on film.

In 1956, Kaye toured as the UNICEF ambassador, which was featured on the *See It Now* television show. In 1963, Kaye was offered his own television show, *The*

Danny Kaye Show on CBS, which ran from 1963 to 1967. Kaye devoted his life to UNICEF and worked tirelessly to ensure the foundation received the recognition it deserved. Kaye's name became synonymous with UNICEF and, in 1965, when the foundation received the Noble Peace Prize, Kaye was selected to accept the award on behalf of the organization.

Throughout the 1960s and 1970s, Kaye continued performing on television, guest-starring in many of the most popular shows of the time. In 1964, Kaye was badly burned in a kitchen accident but went on to perform his show, doing most of his lines from a wheelchair which was hidden from view with clever camera angles.

Along with Kaye's passion for performing, he enjoyed entertaining and was a master chef. While touring the Orient, Kaye learned to master Chinese cuisine and enjoyed serving exotic dishes for his guests.

In 1977, Kaye became the original owner of the Seattle Mariners baseball team, indulging in another of his passions. He sold his interest in the team in 1981 but was a master of baseball trivia knowledge.

In 1980, an elderly Kaye played in an episode of *The Cosby Show* as the family dentist to great laughs. In the following year, Kaye was finally able to show his true acting ability with a starring role in the film *Skokie* about a survivor of the Nazi concentration camps.

In 1983, Kaye underwent surgery for a quadruple bypass; during this operation, Kaye received a tainted blood transfusion and acquired hepatitis.

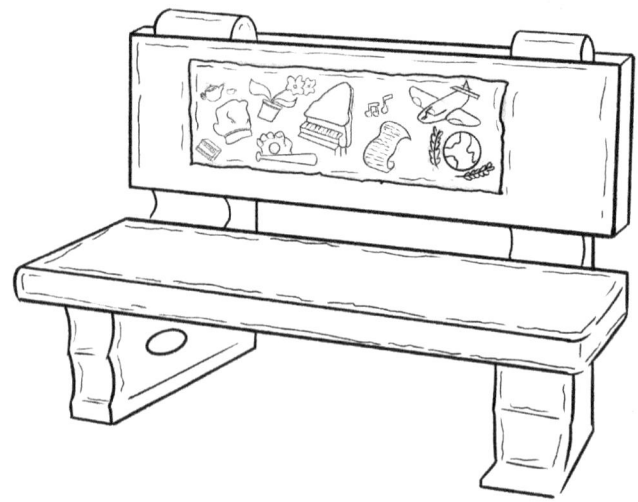

Kaye died of a heart attack on March 3, 1987, at the age of 74. After a private service, Kaye was interred at Kensico Cemetery in Valhalla, New York. Adorning his gravesite is a bench with a bronze plaque showing a baseball and baseball bat, a piano, airplane, musical notes, and a glove; this glove shows Kaye's name with his birth and death dates.

Donald O'Connor

Donald David Dixon Ronald O'Connor was born on August 28, 1925, to Effie and Edward O'Connor in Chicago, Illinois. O'Connor was born into a show business family; his parent were circus performers for Ringling Brothers before going into Vaudeville and becoming stars of the stage.

O'Connor was the fourth child having a sister Arline who was killed by an automobile when O'Connor was only ten months old. O'Connor's father was distraught by his child's deaths and passed away only weeks later of a heart attack, leaving Effie to raise her small family alone.

The family toured the country, sometimes performing for food and board. O'Connor became a part of the act soon after he learned to walk.

In 1937 at the age of twelve, O'Connor was performing on the stage and was offered a part in the

Paramount Pictures production of *Sing You Sinners* starring Bing Crosby. Over the next two years, O'Connor was cast in eleven productions, including *Beau Geste* and *Men With Wings*. This stream of motion pictures seemed never-ending to O'Connor until 1939, when his acting career was put on hold. O'Connor went back to vaudeville with his mother and siblings after his older brother Bill died suddenly.

Over the next three years, the family toured extensively, enjoying modest success on the stage. Finally, in 1942, O'Connor was offered a contract with Universal Studios in a dancing troupe called The Jivin' Jack and Jill's. The studio worked the ensemble tirelessly, producing a string of pictures before O'Connor's eighteenth birthday.

With the start of World War II, O'Connor was drafted into the army when he turned eighteen, but his film career continued even in his absence. While in the Army, O'Connor entertained the troops and never saw real danger during the war.

Finally finished with his service in 1947, O'Connor went back to the studio and starred in *Something For the Wind* costarring Deanna Durbin. Throughout the rest of the 1940s, O'Connor was cast in several movie musicals but never received the breakout role that would make him a star. Finally, in 1949, O'Connor was cast in the film *Francis the Talking Mule,* the story of a soldier who is befriended by a talking mule. The film proved very profitable for Universal, who made six sequels with O'Connor in the lead role.

In 1952, O'Connor was finally given the role of his dreams, starring opposite Gene Kelly in the blockbuster film *Singing in the Rain,* co-starring newcomer Debbie Reynolds. In the role of Cosmo Brown, O'Connor was able to showcase his physically dancing abilities and acrobatic expertise. In the scene for the musical number *Make 'Em Laugh*, O'Connor performed backflips, Somersaults, and running up walls to the point where he was required to be under a doctor's care for several days after the scene was shot.

O'Connor received the Golden Globe® that year for best actor. After the film's success, O'Connor was in high demand, performed in big-budget musicals, and worked on television. When O'Connor was signed on to emcee *The Colgate Comedy Hour*, he finally received the recognition he had always worked for. O'Connor also took the lead role in the film *The Buster Keaton Story*, showing his aptitude to do dramatic work as well as sing and dance.

With the close of the 1950s, Keaton found fewer and fewer roles being offered to him but discovered a new audience when he went back to his roots and started performing on the stage in Las Vegas. Modest success followed O'Connor in Vegas with his ability to take the audience back to an era of song and dance that was almost forgotten. Unfortunately for O'Connor, he found himself in a world where liquor proved too tempting for the aging celebrity. By the end of the 1960s, O'Connor had a significant drinking problem that affected his life on and off the stage.

By the early 1970s, O'Connor's alcoholism affected his performances on the stage, and he was released from his contract. O'Connor finally picked himself up and got the help he needed to beat his demons, finally giving up drinking.

In 1981, O'Connor appeared in the film *Ragtime*, based on the novel by author E. L. Doctorow. O'Connor continued working in film and television throughout the 1980s and 1990s, with his last feature film being *Out To Sea* starring Jack Lemmon and Walter Matthau.

In 2003, O'Connor died of congestive heart failure at his home in Calabasas, California. Surrounded by family, his last words were, "I'd like to thank the Academy for my lifetime achievement award that I will eventually get." Later, O'Connor received the award posthumously.

While known internationally throughout his career, the death of O'Connor was a quiet affair, the family had him cremated, and the remains were given to his wife. No public memorial was offered, and the star was quietly remembered by friends, family, and fans.

Red Skelton

Born Richard Bernard Skelton, the son of a circus clown, Skelton never knew his father, who died only a few months before Skelton's birth. Living in Vincennes, Indiana, Skelton grew up with his mother, Ida, and three older brothers. At the age of ten, Skelton went to work selling newspapers on street corners to help his family financially. One day while selling in front of Pantheon Theater, he sold a paper to Vaudeville performer Ed Wynn. Wynn took the young boy backstage and introduced him to the other performers in the show. Skelton found he had been bitten by the acting bug, wanting to learn more about the world on the stage. By the time Skelton was fifteen years old, he had left home and hit the road working anywhere he could find a job as an entertainer. Riverboats, Mistral shows, Medicine Shows, even the same circus where his father had performed so many years earlier gave Skelton the chance to show off his comedy skills for adoring audiences.

In 1930, Skelton worked in Kansas City, Kansas, and met a young dancer named Edna Stillwell. They developed a Vaudeville act and began touring together throughout the Midwest and Canada. The duo married and maintained a partnership together for thirteen years before divorcing.

In 1938, Skelton received his first break into the world of radio and film. He was offered a role in the film *Having a Wonderful Time* starring Ginger Rogers and Douglas Fairbanks Jr. Throughout the 1940s and 1950s, Skelton performed in over thirty films like *Whistling in Dixie* and *Panama Hattie* starring Ann Rutherford, *The Show Off* with Marjorie Main, and *Three Little Words* opposite Fred Astaire and Vera Ellen.

In 1941, Skelton was offered his own radio show, *The Raleigh Cigarette Program.* It was here that Skelton showcased his comedic side with sketches consisting of characters like Willie Lump Lump, Clem Kadiddlehopper, and Cauliflower McPugg. Throughout World War II, Skelton sold war bonds on his show to help the war effort and show his patriotism.

In 1944, Skelton was drafted into the United States Army, being shipped overseas to do his duty for his country. The radio show was put on hold, but Skelton was not made for military work, having a nervous breakdown in Italy and discharged only months later. The show resumed in 1945, continuing till 1949 when Skelton decided to move his radio show to CBS.

In 1951, Skelton was asked to bring his show to television by NBC, and Skelton jumped at the chance to bring his characters to life on the small screen. Skelton introduced his best-known character, Freddie the Freeloader, a loveable clown/tramp on the show with six-minute sketches each week. He enjoyed great success with the show until the spring of 1953 when the program was canceled due to declining ratings. Skelton took the show to CBS in 1953 and remained with the network until 1970.

Skelton purchased an old theater in Hollywood on La Brea Avenue once owned by Charlie Chaplin and converted the antique equipment to be used with color film. Skelton became the first television show to be filmed and shown in color. Skelton attempted to convince the studios to start airing color television shows, but the studio heads were reluctant to change the format of already popular shows from black and white.

In 1957, Skelton's nine-year-old son was diagnosed with Leukemia, and the boy died shortly after his diagnosis. Skelton was devastated, and the 1957-58 season of his show was shown with guest hosts as the comedian could not bring himself to perform his comedy. The show continued until 1970, when the studio decided to cancel the program due to lower ratings and soaring production costs. Skelton was very embittered by this and felt CBS had stabbed him in the back after so many profitable years.

During the 1970s, Skelton went back to his performing roots and began touring the United States nightclubs and casinos. It was also during this time that

Skelton went back to another passion, painting. Skelton's clown paintings began as a mere hobby but were so well received that his art brought eighty thousand dollars for each piece.

While he continued working in film and television as a guest artist, Skelton semi-retired to his art and family, moving to Rancho Mirage, California, to enjoy his golden years in peace. Skelton raised quarter horses, loving the animals throughout his lifetime.

Skelton died of pneumonia on September 17, 1997, at Eisenhower Medical Center, surrounded by family and friends. After a private funeral service, Skelton was interred in the Great Mausoleum at Forest Lawn Memorial Park in Glendale, California, in a private family mausoleum along with his son Richard who died in 1958. Among the Hollywood royalty buried alongside Skelton are Jean Harlow, theater owner Sid Grauman and studio head Irving Thalberg.

Fanny Brice

Fanny Brice was born Fania Borach in New York City on October 29, 1891. The third child of her mother, Rose Stern, and her father, Charles Borach, the couple own a series of saloons in New York. Borach allowed his daughter to sing and dance for his customers, and Brice found her calling as an entertainer. Her mother worked the saloon while her husband drank and played cards with the patrons. Finally fed up with the arrangement, Stern sold off the chain of saloons and took her children to Brooklyn, where she sold real estate.

At the age of thirteen, Brice dropped out of school to begin performing in the chorus at a local house of burlesque. A year later, Brice found her way to the Broadway stage in the revue *The College Girls* and found great success singing "Sadie Salome, Go Home" with her Yiddish accent. Ironically enough, Brice did not speak a word of Yiddish, but the accent fit the stereotypical Jewish girl for the show.

In 1911, while still in her teens, Brice met local barber Frank White while touring in Springfield, Massachusetts, and the two were married. They were married for only three years before Brice filed for divorce and moved on with the show and her career.

Trying marriage again in 1918, Brice married local con man and thief, Jules "Nicky" Arnstein. Brice stayed with Arnstein during his prison sentence at Sing Sing Prison and through several infidelities during their marriage. In 1924, Arnstein was brought up on Wall Street securities theft charges and went into hiding, leaving Brice to withstand the media harassment alone. Even with Arnstein's cowardice, Brice stood by his side, paying for his legal counsel expenses. Brice worked continuously to pay for her husband's many indiscretions, which drained her earnings on the stage.

Even though Brice put everything she had into his defense, Arnstein went to prison once again, leaving Brice and their two children behind. Upon his release in 1927, Arnstein disappeared without a word to Brice, and she finally divorced him. In 1941, Arnstein tried to reconcile with Brice only to find she was too smart to become involved with him a second time.

During the late 1920s, Brice tried her hand at serious drama, becoming tired of the comedic Jewish roles she was given. Each of the dramas she was cast in were failures, and Brice finally gave up on her dream of becoming a serious actress and went back to comedy.

When she was nineteen years old, Brice found her fondness for humor and became an accomplished comedienne. It was only two years later, in 1921, that she met the great Florenz Zigfield, who hired Brice on the spot. For the next twenty years, Brice was a headline entertainer with the Zigfield Follies in New York City. Her debut was singing the popular song *Lovey Joe* in the 1910 Follies. In 1921, Brice was given the song *My Man* to sing in the show. Little did she dream that this would become her signature song for the rest of her career. Another song associated with Brice throughout her life would be the tune *Second Hand Rose* which became a popular hit during the 1920s. Brice toured with the Follies, developing new characters like "The Vamp" and "The Pretentious Dancer" but was best known for her character of "The Blushing Bride."

In 1938, Brice was offered her own radio show and quickly took the offer. It was here that Brice was able to show a broader audience her gift of dialects and accents. Her most popular character was the Baby Snooks, a whiny toddler that charmed her weekly audience. Her radio show lasts until she died in 1951, offering her great success for many years. Even though the show was only heard on the radio, it is said that Brice donned a toddler costume during the show to channel the character. Baby Snooks was only seen once on television on the 1950 CBS show *Popsicle Parade of Stars;* this was the only television appearance Brice would make during her career.

Soon after the appearance on *Parade of Stars*, Brice died suddenly of a cerebral hemorrhage on May 29, 1951, at fifty-nine. That night she was scheduled to do her radio show, and the broadcast became an on-air memorial to the great comedienne. Co-star Henry Stafford offered a brief eulogy for Brice when he said:

"We have lost a very real, a very warm, a very wonderful woman."

Brice was cremated and interred at Home of Peace Cemetery in Los Angeles, California. Fifty years later, upon the death of Brice's daughter Frances, her remains were removed and placed at Westwood Memorial Park in an outdoor garden near her daughter's grave.

In 1964, Singer Barbara Streisand portrayed Brice in the Broadway production of *Funny Girl*, a loosely based biography of her Zigfield years, to great acclaim. In 1968, Streisand won the Academy Award® after reprising the role in the film version of the show.

Red Buttons

Born Aaron Chwatt in New York City to a Jewish immigrant family on February 5, 1919. Red Buttons is known for his shocking red hair and comedy style and his Academy Award® winning dramatic work.

Button's began performing on street corners in New York for pennies at the age of seven. His beautiful baritone voice allowed him to sing with the Cooperman's choir for the next three years, honing his performance skills. Buttons performed for audiences at local talent shows and amateur contests. Growing up during the Great Depression, the prize money was always a welcome sight in the Buttons family.

At the age of sixteen, Buttons began working as a bellhop at a local tavern in the Bronx for a steady paycheck. The tavern's bandleader, who found Buttons red hair and shiny buttoned uniform humorous, began calling the young man Red Buttons and the name stuck. That summer, Buttons was paired with Robert Alda, a Vaudeville singer, and dancer. The pair became a comedy team, with Alda as the straight man and Buttons bringing the comedy. By 1939, Buttons was working at the famed Minsky's Burlesque in Manhattan. Two years later, actor Jose Ferrer discovered Buttons and offered him a part in the Broadway show *The Admiral Had a Wife*. Buttons took the role but never had the opportunity to perform as the show was based on the Navy base in Pearl Harbor, Hawaii and the theater owners felt it would be in bad taste after the Japanese bombing on December 7, 1941. Later, Buttons said the only reason the Japanese bombed Pearl Harbor was to keep him off-Broadway.

The next year, Buttons would get another chance on Broadway in the show *Vickie*. That same year, Buttons went back to Minsky's to perform one last time. As fate would have it, the club was raided while Buttons was on stage, and the local authorities closed the club forever due to changing laws about immorality.

In 1943, Buttons was drafted and performed in the show *Winged Victory* for the troops during World War II. Buttons also performed on the European stage with a young Mickey Rooney. After the war, Buttons went right back to Broadway, performing in several successful shows.

In 1952, Buttons was offered his own television series, *The Red Buttons Show,* which ran for three years and received great ratings and critical acclaim. Buttons even won the Academy of Radio and Television Arts and Science Award in 1952; this award would later be known as the Emmy®.

In 1957, Buttons showed a different side of his acting skills with a dramatic role in the film *Sayonara* starring Marlon Brando and co-starring Josh Logan. Buttons won the Academy Award® for Best Supporting Actor and a Golden Globe® for Best Supporting Actor for his performance of a young soldier married to a Japanese girl, but the United States government would not recognize their marriage during the war. Ultimately Buttons and his co-star commit suicide, finding no other way to be together.

Buttons career took off, and he became a full-blown movie star. A string of successful pictures followed with roles in *The Big Circus, Imitation General,* and *Hatari!* allowing Buttons to settle in as one of the Hollywood elite. Once again, in 1956, Buttons was nominated for his role in the film *Harlow*, a biography of the great blonde bombshell who died tragically at a young age.

With television becoming a hot new medium, Buttons performed guest appearances of many of the popular shows of the day, like *GE True Theater* and *Frontier Circus*. The 1960s proved Buttons to be a talent that would continue through the decades. From *The Longest Day* to *Your Cheatin' Heart*, Buttons showed a range of performances little seen by other comedians.

The 1970s brought a new generation of Buttons fans with roles in blockbusters like *The Poseidon Adventure* and *The Sunshine Boys,* co-starring Lionel Stander, and Bella Bruck. Buttons continued working increasingly through the 1980s with guest appearances on television shows like *Rosanne, Family Law,* and a reoccurring role on the medical series *E.R.*

Buttons finally died on July 13, 2006, at the age of eighty-seven. Surrounded by family and friends, Buttons suffered from vascular disease for months before his death. Buttons was quietly cremated without fanfare or a public memorial, and his remains were given to his children.

Abbott & Costello

Bud Abbott and Lou Costello were known throughout the world as the archetype of American comedy. Spanning every genre of entertainment from Burlesque, radio, film, and television, there is no other comedy duo better known or more loved than these two comedy greats.

William Alexander Abbott was born on October 2, 1897, in Ashbury Park, New Jersey, to a show business family. Abbott's parents, Rae & Harry, worked for the Barnum and Bailey circus, his mother a bareback rider and his father a forage agent.

Abbott dropped out of school as a young boy and started working at Coney Island in New York in 1909. By the time he was sixteen, Abbott's father had employed his son at the Casino Theater in Brooklyn, working in the box office. It was here that Abbott learned how to work with acts and became proficient in how to manage the Vaudeville acts that came to town. Abbott soon began putting together Vaudeville tours and managing entire shows. During this time, he met a young dancer named Betty Smith, who would later become his wife. The two were married in 1918 and began touring together, Abbott as the straight man to Betty's comedy. By 1924, the couple developed their own show, *Broadway Flashes,* and Abbott was invited to work with such great comedians as Harry Evanson and Harry Steppe.

By the early 1903s, Abbott was performing at Minsky's Burlesque when he met a young comic named Lou Costello. The two men respected one another's talent but didn't work together for a few more years.

Lou Costello was born Louis Francis Cristillo in Paterson, New Jersey, on March 6, 1906. As a child, Costello enjoyed sports and excelled at basketball, becoming the foul shot champion of New Jersey. He also tried his hand at boxing under the name "Lou King" but preferred the stage to the boxing ring and gave up fighting to perform comedy.

In 1924, Costello came to Hollywood to work in silent films but struggled to find work. He worked at the studio as a set laborer and as an extra but could not get the roles he wanted. In 1930, finally discouraged and in the throes of the Great Depression, Costello left Hollywood to make his way back to New York but did not have any money for the trip. Costello worked his way east, hitchhiking along the way, and ran out of money in Saint Joseph, Missouri. It was here that Costello found work in a local burlesque theater as a comic and eventually made enough money to fund the rest of his trip back to New York.

Finally, back on familiar ground, Costello found work at local theaters and burlesque houses. Finally, in 1936, Costello worked with his straight man, who suddenly fell ill, and Abbott happened to be on hand to substitute. The two found great chemistry and began working together touring vaudeville, minstrel shows, and burlesque houses.

Their first years together were difficult, and work was hard to find. Still suffering the after-effects of the great depression, the team continued knocking on doors until they met Ted Collins, manager of singer Kate Smith. Abbott and Costello asked if they could appear on *The Kate Smith Radio Show,* and the team became the summer replacement act to massive success. They continued working on radio and on Broadway in shows like *Streets of Paris,* finding audiences loving their brand of comedy.

During this time, Abbott and Costello, along with comedy writer John Grant created a comedy sketch that would rocket the team to international fame and become the best-known act in comedy history, "Who's on First," a bit where Abbott tried to explain the names of a baseball team with Costello becoming confused and increasingly frustrated with his partner. This became their signature act, getting them the attention all the way to the west coast in Hollywood.

In 1939, Abbott and Costello were signed to a contract with Universal Pictures, and their first film, *One Night in the Tropics,* became their test to see if the men would win the movie audience like they did the theater audience. Not only did the movie-going public love them, but the crew on set also laughed so hard during filming they struggled to get most of the shots completed. The studio knew they had a hit team and began cranking out Abbott and Costello films like *Buck Privates, In the Navy, Hold that Ghost,* and *Abbott & Costello Meet Frankenstein.* A total of thirty-six films were made with the team from 1939 to 1957.

Abbott and Costello branched out during their movie career to appear in their weekly television show on ABC *The Abbotts and Costello Show* from 1941 to 1946 and then on NBC from 1946 to 1949.

During the height of their popularity, the team went across the country selling war bonds and raised Eighty-five million dollars for the war effort. After the tour, Costello came down with Rheumatic fever and was bedridden for almost a year. The day Costello was scheduled to return to the radio show, his infant son died in a tragic accident, but he still went on that night as scheduled. Abbott later said about his partner; He epitomized the phrase "The Show Must Go On."

In 1956, just before releasing their last film, *Dance with me Henry*, the team decided to retire and announced their split. Abbott was aging and needed to slow down in his later years. That same year, Abbott and Costello were inducted into The Baseball Hall of Fame in Cooperstown, New York, the only non-baseball celebrities to have this honor in its history.

Even though his partner was older, Costello passed away first after a heart attack on March 3, 1959, three days short of his fifty-third birthday. It was said that Costello suffered a heart attack that put him in the hospital. He was visited by his agent, who snuck in an ice-cream soda at the request of the sick man. Once finished with the treat, Costello uttered, "That was the best ice-cream soda I ever tasted." Immediately after the words were said, Costello suffered another massive heart attack and died.

The funeral for Costello was attended by most of the comedy royalty of the 1950s. Red Skelton, Joe E. Brown and Danny Thomas, and partner Bud Abbott led the pallbearers to Costello's final resting place at Calvary Cemetery in Los Angeles, Ca.

Abbott outlived his partner by almost fifteen years, dying on April 24, 1974, losing his battle to cancer after living out his last years in quiet seclusion after suffering two strokes. The great straight man was quietly cremated, and his remains scattered in the Pacific Ocean.

Morey Amsterdam

Comedian and writer Morey Amsterdam was born Moritz Amsterdam on December 14, 1908. The youngest of three sons, Amsterdam became the straight man for his older brothers and, by 1922, began working in Vaudeville with his older siblings. A little-known fact about Amsterdam, he became an accomplished cellist and used this musical talent throughout his career on the stage.

During the prohibition years, Amsterdam worked in a speakeasy owned by the notorious gangster Al Capone. One night while on the job, Amsterdam was caught in the middle of a gunfight and decided to head west to find a new career.

Moving on with new ventures, Amsterdam began working as a comedy writer. Amsterdam was dubbed by his fellow comedians as "The Human Joke Machine," a moniker he wore proudly. Amsterdam strapped a machine to his chest and hand crank it with a long strip of paper expelled from the machine. He read the joke to the audience to thunderous laughter and applause.

Amsterdam became a household name with his first appearance on the radio program *The Al Pearce Show* and soon was the master of ceremonies for *The Night Club of the Air* show in 1937. By 1947, Amsterdam appeared on multiple radio shows simultaneously, *The Morey Amsterdam Show* and *Stop me if You've Heard This One,* just two of the many shows that showcased his talent. CBS turned Amsterdam's namesake show into a weekly television series with the show running on both mediums for a time with the same script and cast for both shows.

Amsterdam was an act made for television, and he hosted *Broadway Open House* on NBC, which was the predecessor to *The Tonight Show*. Amsterdam appeared on several of the new shows and continue his radio success, making him one of the highest-paid entertainers of the 1940s.

It was not until 1961 that Amsterdam would take on the role that would define him for generations and rocket him into stardom. *The Dick Van Dyke Show* ran from 1961 through 1966 with Amsterdam playing Buddy Sorrell, a part recommended to him by a long-time friend Rose Marie who played opposite him as a television writer. The duo created perfect comedic timing opposite Van Dyke, and the show was a hit with audiences.

During the 1960s, Amsterdam appeared in several Beach Party films produced by his own company, American International Pictures. He also appeared in the film, *Don't Worry, We'll Think of a Title Later,* written by Amsterdam.

With the approach of the 1970s, Amsterdam's career slowed, and he worked on and off, even becoming a panelist for the game show *Match Game* for a time. Later, He and his friend Rose Marie worked together on *Hollywood Squares* as a duo.

In the 1990s, Amsterdam appeared on several episodes of the soap opera *The Young and the Restless,* and his final television appearance was on the 1996 show *Caroline in the City* with Rose Marie.

Soon after his final television appearance, Amsterdam died of a massive heart attack. The funeral of Amsterdam was held at University Synagogue and was a who's who of early comedy. Milton Berle, Steve Allen, Red Buttons, and Rose Marie were just a few of his friends in attendance. Jan Murray gave the eulogy to tearful laughter. He claimed that *"When Amsterdam died, he was the size of a cufflink." "We shrink as we get older, ya know."*

Amsterdam was buried at Forest Lawn Memorial Park in the Hollywood Hills in the outdoor mausoleum. His epitaph reads, "He gave the world 74 years of comedy and entertainment".

Mae West

The notorious bad girl of the cinema, Mae West, made her mark on stage, screen, and society with her flamboyant, scandalous personality. Her in your face sexuality made men adore her, and women want to be her. Not only an accomplished actress on stage and screen but well known and respected as a writer and comedienne West became the face of all that was naughty in Hollywood.

Mae West was born Mary Jane West on August 17, 1893, to a corset model and private detective. West began performing at church socials at the age of five and, by the age of seven, was performing in amateur contests singing and dancing, often winning first prize. By the time she was fourteen, West was playing vaudeville with the Hal Clarendon Stock Company trying her hand at various characters, including a male impersonator.

On April 11, 1911, West was married to fellow Vaudevillian Frank Wallace, but the couple kept their marriage a secret for professional reasons. It was not until 1937 that West finally admitted to being married when a clerk discovered the marriage certificate. While never living together as man and wife, the two remained married until 1942, when West finally filed for divorce.

By 1911, West was performing as a dancer on Broadway in the revue *A La Broadway*. Even though the show ran for only eight performances, West was noticed by the New York Times and was cast in *Vera Violetta's* show starring Al Jolson.

West's mother was her biggest fan, always encouraging her daughter to perform and telling her whatever she tried was terrific. Unfortunately for West, her mother was the minority opinion in the family. Her grandmother and aunt disapproved of her choice to be a performer and especially disapproved of West's choices of material in her act later in her career. Her family's disapproval did not stop West from continuing on the path to stardom, using her sexuality as a springboard.

By 1918, West played the lead role in the Broadway revue, *Sometimes* opposite veteran comedian Ed Wynn. West performed the provocative dance "the shimmy" in the show to a shocked audience. West was encouraged to write her explicit plays, so she wrote, directed, and starred in the play *Sex*. While the reviewers had nothing good to say about the play, the ticket sales were good, but the show closed after a police raid on the theater. On April 19, 1927, West was prosecuted on moral's charges and sentenced to ten days in jail for "Corrupting the morals of youth."

While the city was trying to make an example of West and discourage public acceptance of her theater performances, the plan backfired when West told reporters of her wearing silk underpants and dining with the warden and his wife during her eight days in jail. West's sentence was reduced by two days for good behavior, and her career soared with the opening of her next play, *The Drag*. They ran the play in Connecticut and Vermont to good reviews, but when she tried to open the play in New York, The Society for the Prevention of Vice threatened to ban the show. All this did was keep West on the front page of the newspaper and offer free publicity for her next three plays. In 1928, her play *Diamond Lil* was a smash hit on Broadway; with her playing the lead role, the character became her signature persona for the rest of her career.

In 1930, West's mother died, leaving her daughter grief-stricken. West moved to Los Angeles and took an apartment at the Ravenswood Hotel, where she lived for the rest of her life.

At the age of thirty-eight, West was offered a contract with Paramount Pictures and began acting opposite George Raft and a young newcomer to Hollywood, Cary Grant. In the 1933 film, *She Done Him Wrong,* West played opposite Grant in his first major film role and shot him to instant stardom. By 1933, West was the highest-paid person in America next to William Randolph Hearst and enjoyed all the Hollywood lifestyle had to offer. West continued to work for Paramount until 1937. Each of her films became more challenging to produce due to a crackdown by the Production code to edit any inappropriate content. West's films began to suffer, and the studio ended the relationship in 1937 after her last film, *Every Days a Holiday.*

After West parted ways with the studios, she found her career fading, so she went to radio appearing on *The Chase and Sanborn Hour,* playing opposite Edgar Bergen and his puppet Charlie McCarthy. West claimed McCarthy's kisses gave her splinters and made suggestive references to him being made from wood. Another risqué sketch involved actor Don Ameche playing opposite West as Adam and Eve in the garden of Eden. The studio was flooded with mail claiming the show was immoral and obscene. The Federal Communications Commission later reported the broadcast as "vulgar and indecent." NBC took the opportunity to throw West under the bus claiming it was not the script but the inflection in her voice that gave the air of suggestiveness to the sketch. West left NBC and never appear on another radio program until 1950.

In 1939, Universal Pictures offered West a role opposite funnyman W.C. Fields. After an eighteen-month hiatus from film, West took the role of Flower Bell Lee in *My Little Chickadee,* which became her most iconic movie role. West and Fields instantly disliked each other on the set and fought over the screenplay throughout filming. The film was a huge box office success garnering West a reprieve with audiences and boosting her career once more. West performed in her last film in 1943 for Columbia Pictures. *The Heat's On* opened to terrible reviews and was a bust at the box office. West returned to New York and the Broadway theater, giving up on Hollywood altogether.

Upon her return to the theater, West played *Catherine the Great* in a comedic spoof produced by

Mike Todd, the ex-husband of actress Elizabeth Taylor. The show was a huge success, and West found herself surrounded by young bodybuilders as her imperial guard on stage. Enjoying this so much, West created a Las Vegas show for herself and hired a bevy of muscular men to carry her around on stage. One of her actors, Mickey Hargitay, would go on to marry bombshell Jayne Mansfield and it was rumored that West was furious for losing one of her boys to the rival actress.

In 1959, West wrote her autobiography *Goodness had Nothing to do with It,* which became a best seller. During the 1960s, West appeared on the occasional television series and recorded two albums, *Way Out West* and *Wild Christmas.*

In 1970, West returned to the movie screen once more in Gore Vidal's *Myra Breckinridge,* costarring Raquel Welch, Farrah Fawcett, and newcomer Tom Selleck. The film was a box office disaster, and Vidal was later quoted saying it was "an awful joke." Even with the financial disaster of Breckinridge, it went on to video becoming a cult classic with newer generations. In 1978, West would appear in her last film *Sextette.* In her eighties, West appeared disoriented, and most of her scenes were filmed from her waist up to hide the production assistant guiding her through her scenes. Her failing eyesight caused her to have a microphone concealed inside her wig, with an assistant feeding her the lines throughout filming. The film once again bombed at the theaters and would be the final nail in the coffin of West's career in Hollywood.

In August 1980, West suffered a stroke that left her bedridden and hospitalized for months. During her stay in the hospital, West suffered from an allergic reaction to the feeding tube solution, which caused a second severe stroke, and additional health complications. In November 1980, West was finally released from the hospital to return to her home, but her health did not improve.

Finally, on November 22, 1980, West died at her home, sitting in an armchair in her guest bedroom.

The private funeral for West was held at the Old North Church at Forest Lawn Hollywood Hills on November 25, 1980. Critic Kevin Thomas said while giving the eulogy, *"the woman and the legend have long since become one."*

MAE WEST

1893 — 1980

West's body was shipped back to New York and interred in the family crypt in Cypress Hills Cemetery in Brooklyn, New York. The notoriety and scandalous nature which followed West throughout her life have continued to keep her memory alive, enticing future generations to enjoy the bawdy blondes' antics throughout the decades.

Phil Silvers

Known as the King of Chutzpah, Phil Silvers is known as one of his generation's greatest comedy entertainers. With his horn-rimmed glasses and toothy grin, he coined the catchphrase "Gladaseeya!" (glad to see you).

On May 11, 1911, Silvers was born in Brooklyn, New York, to Russian-Jewish immigrants. The youngest of eight children, Silvers learned early to get the attention he needed with a good act. By the age of eleven, Silvers was singing in local theaters after an incident when the projector broke down during a flicker. Silvers left school at the age of thirteen to pursue a career as a comedian's stooge.

Silvers toured in Vaudeville and burlesque houses appearing as a singer and comedian. He finally landed a part in the short-lived play *Yokel Boy* in New York, where he charmed audiences with his comic timing. The critics raved about Silvers's performance in an otherwise bad play which encouraged Silvers to head out west to try his luck at motion pictures.

Silvers made his film debut in *The Hit Parade of 1941,* starring Kenny Bake and Frances Langford. Silvers worked for MGM, Columbia, and 20th Century Fox studios over the next two decades playing the same vaudeville-style comedy he perfected on the stage. When the studio began to look to newer comedians for their films and he was not at the top of their list anymore, Silvers moved back to New York and his roots on the stage.

With the invention of television in the 1950s, Silvers jumped at the chance to perform his comedy for a national audience and was cast as Sergeant Ernest G. Bilko in *You'll Never Get Rich,* later retitle to *The Phil Silvers Show.* The show ran for four years, from 1955 to 1959, winning Silvers several Emmy® awards. The show was canceled not due to a decline in ratings but due to the enormous budget required to maintain the ensemble cast.

Silvers returned to films in the classic *It's a Mad Mad Mad Mad World* and in the Marilyn Monroe film, *Something's Got to Give.* In 1963, Silvers reinvented *The Phil Silvers Show* and took advantage of his reclaimed fame to appear in motion pictures in the U.S. and abroad. Silvers was offered the lead role in the Broadway play *A Funny Thing Happened on the Way to the Forum* in 1962 but turned it down, the part going to veteran actor Zero Mostel. The show was a huge success, and Mostel reprised his role for the movie version of the play. Silvers agreed to appear in the film version in a supporting role in 1966, kicking himself for his error in judgment.

Silvers was finally allowed to play the lead in *Forum* in 1972 when Larry Blyden offered him the role in the revival on Broadway. Silvers won a Tony® award for his performance, the first actor to ever win the honor for a revival show.

That same year, Silvers suffered a stroke, leaving him with permanently slurred speech. This did not deter Silvers from performing, and he went on to work on television with a cameo on *Happy Days* and *Fantasy Island*. These would be the last time Silver's would be seen to a viewing audience.

Silvers' health continued to decline, and the great comedian finally died of a heart attack on November 1, 1985. In his will, Silvers made several requests. First, long-time friend Milton Berle give the Eulogy. Second, the funeral arrangements, coffin, and headstone should not exceed ten thousand dollars, and finally, the funeral be held at Forest Lawn Memorial Park in Hollywood Hills.

Silvers' wishes were granted, and he was buried at Mount Sinai Memorial park in Hollywood, California. The simple headstone reads "Phil Silvers Comedian."

Imogene Coca

Most recognizable for her comedy with Side Cesar in *Your Show of Shows*, Imogene Coca became one of the first ladies of comedy with her round eyes, puzzle smirk, and ever-present laughter.

Imogene Coca was born Imogene Fernandez De Coca on November 18, 1908, in Philadelphia, Pennsylvania, to a Vaudeville family. Her father, a violinist and orchestra conductor, her mother a dancer and magician's assistant.

Coca started performing at a very young age taking piano, dancing, and singing lessons. Wanting to become a serious dancer, Coca studied ballet and found herself employed as a full-time acrobat in Vaudeville alongside her parents by the age of thirteen.

While still a teenager, Coca left her family and traveled to New York to dance on Broadway. Fate would lend a hand getting her first dancing role in the musical

When you Smile and Coca soon became a headliner in the Manhattan night clubs. For the next thirty years, Coca plied her talents, singing and dancing but soon found an affinity for comedy, adding bits of pantomime through the years. One night while working on the show *New Faces of 1935* with Leonard Tillman, Coca wore an oversized coat to keep warm in the chilly theater. She and several male dancers began leaping around, improvising dance steps. Tillman encouraged the group to repeat the performance that night on the stage, and they reluctantly agreed. The audience laughed and applauded, the critics crediting Coca for the comedic routine.

To refine her comedy style, Coca began working in the Poconos mountains of New York with the likes of Danny Kaye and Carol Channing during the summers of 1935 to 1939. Coca struggled to find work as a comedienne but continued her stage act dancing for the vacationers visiting the resorts. Finally, in 1949, she was offered a role on *The Admiral Broadway Revue* opposite Sid Cesar. NBC received great reviews for the show and the next year launched *Your Show of Shows* with Coca and Cesar headlining. Coca won her first Emmy® award for her portrayal of Doris Hickenlooper. Coca and Cesar left the show the next year to branch out in solo careers, Coca premiering *The Imogene Coca Show,* which lasted only one season. Coca and Cesar paired again for *Sid Cesar Invites You* but some of the original magic was lost, and the show was canceled, the network citing low viewership. *Your Show of Shows'* original cast returned to reprise their roles in 1967 and won an Emmy® for an outstanding variety show.

In 1973, Coca suffered major injuries when she was in a car accident with her second husband, King Donovan. Coca lost the sight in her right eye in the accident, Donovan suffered only minor injuries while the rear-view mirror smashed coca's cheekbone. After plastic surgery and a lens to cover her blind eye, she continued working intermittently on stage with her old partner; Cesar revamped most of their old routines for new audiences through 1991.

Coca continued working on television, guest-starring on most of the popular programs like *The Carol Burnette Show, It's About Time,* and *The Dick Cavett Show.* Coca found a new younger audience when she took the role of aunt Edna in the wildly popular 1983 comedy film *National Lampoon's Vacation* starring Chevy Chase and Beverly DeAngelo.

Coca finally retired and was diagnosed with Alzheimer's disease in the late 1990s. She settled in Westport, Connecticut, and, on June 2, 2001, she died of natural causes brought on by the disease. Cesar released this statement after her death.

> *"All the wonderful times we shared meant the world to me. It was a pleasure working with her. I will miss her dearly,"* *Caesar said from his home in Beverly Hills, California.*

One of Coca's final requests was there to be no funeral service. She was quietly cremated, and her remains scattered in an undisclosed location.

Ray Bolger

The wiry dancer who charmed millions as the scarecrow in *The Wizard of Oz*, Ray Bolger's immense talent on stage, screen, and television brought to life the many characters from the funny to the dramatic.

Raymond Wallace Bolger was born January 10, 1904, in Boston, Massachusetts, to Anne and James Edward Bolger. Bolger grew up in Boston, Massachusetts, graduated from high school in 1927. Bolger went to work after graduation, trying his hand as a bank messenger, working for a peanut company, and even working for a life insurance company in the Boston area. While these jobs provided a steady paycheck, the work was unsatisfying for the man who wanted to dance.

It was clear from early childhood that Bolger would become an entertainer. Learning to dance, Bolger found he could move his body unlike other dancers and began to ad-lib moves to showcase his agility. Bolger attended the theater often to watch the Vaudeville acts, studying the actors to acquire new skills he could use later.

Bolger paired with another dancer to form the duo Sanford and Bolger, and the act began touring the country on the Vaudeville circuit.

In 1926, Bolger found himself playing the legendary *Palace Theater* in New York and knew he had arrived in the big time. Soon he began performing on Broadway using his rubber band-like body to charm audiences during his dance numbers.

Bolger was discovered by an MGM talent scout while on stage and was offered a contract with the movie studio. Bolger signed and moved to Los Angeles to begin work in motion pictures. His first film, *The Great Ziegfeld,* starred William Powell and Myrna Loy and showcased another Broadway comedienne Fanny Brice. Bolger's next film *Rosalie* allowed him to show his acting talent opposite dancer Eleanor Powell and Baritone Nelson Eddy.

Bolger continued working as a dancer in bit parts until 1939, when he played a role that would forever change the history of motion pictures.

The Wizard of Oz, starring Judy Garland, showcased Bolger as the scarecrow along with Bert Lahr as the cowardly lion and Jack Haley as the tin man. Bolger was slated to play the tin man but insisted on performing the scarecrow part instead; while the studio heads rejected this change in casting, the eventually conceded and Bolger took on the scarecrow character. Bolger had no way of knowing just how luck he was to change parts, when the makeup used for the tin man character, aluminum power, caused Buddy Ebsen, the original actor who played the tin man, to be hospitalized, and was placed in an iron lung when his lungs were coated with the aluminum powder. Jack Haley was brought on to play the tin man. Bolger's ability to bend his body lent a sense of realism to the scarecrow character, and Bolger's dance sequence during *If I Only Had a Brain* became one of the best-loved in film history. In the original sequence, Bolger created a lengthy choreography dancing along the yellow brick road and bouncing off the fence posts; the scene was cut to include just the singing part and left to the ages until 1998 when the entire footage was included for the theatrical re-release.

During the filming, the makeup worn by Bolger included a prosthetic rubber material that left marks on the actor's skin that did not completely fade for almost a year.

After his film commitments were complete, Bolger headed back east and became a featured act at the Paramount Theater in New York City. Bolger was on stage the night the Japanese bombed Pearl Harbor, and his act was interrupted by President Roosevelt's announcement of the horrific incident.

In 1946, Bolger teamed up again with Garland in the Technicolor musical *The Harvey Girls* costarring John Hodiak and Angela Lansbury. Bolger played a cowardly city man going to the wild west and becomes a blacksmith in Arizona, again showcasing his comedic talents as well as his dancing ability.

With the invention of television, Bolger was invited to guest star on many popular variety shows. In 1954 he was offered his own show, *The Ray Bolger Show,* which featured Bolger along with an ensemble cast dancing, singing, and doing sketch comedy inspired by their years on the stage in Vaudeville. The show only ran for fifty-eight episodes before being canceled.

Throughout the 1960s and 1970s, Bolger continued acting on television and dancing full time. Bolger appeared as a cast addition to the family comedy *The Partridge Family* playing the father to Shirley Jones. Bolger also appeared on the 1970s show *Little House on the Prairie* playing the loveable vagrant Tobey No. His last television appearance was on the 1984 show *Different Strokes* starring Conrad Bain, Dana Plato, and Gary Coleman. The next year Bolger appeared in the dance documentary *That's Dancing* but showed his age during the production.

Bolger was diagnosed with bladder cancer and died on January 15, 1987, at his home in Los Angeles, California, five days after his eighty-third birthday. He was the last surviving member of the original *Wizard of Oz* cast.

The funeral for Bolger was held on Monday, January 19, 1987, at Good Shepherd Catholic Church in Beverly Hills. The private service included family and friends, and after the brief service, his body was taken to Holy Cross Memorial Park in Culver City, California, and interred in the Chapel Mausoleum. A simple epitaph reads Ray Bolger 1904 - 1987.

ZaSu Pitts

The timid, wide-eyed comedienne of radio and motion pictures, ZaSu Pitts, made her mark playing the worrywart to decades of adoring fans.

ZaSu Pitts was born Eliza Susan Pitts in Parsons, Kansas, on January 3, 1894. Her parents, Rulandus and Nellie, raised Pitts and her three siblings in a modest home. Her father lost his leg serving during the Civil War but managed to provide for his family well.

When Pitts was nine years old, the family packed their few belongings and moved to Santa Cruz, California, to find better opportunities and warmer weather. Pitts enjoyed her school years, joining the drama club and performing in many high school plays. After graduation, Pitts continued working in local theater productions, but the lure of Hollywood was beckoning.

Pitts left home and moved to Los Angeles in 1916, at the age of twenty-two, haunting casting offices all over Los Angeles begging for work as an extra on any film. Her first film, *The Little Princess,* gave Pitts an opportunity to work with box office star Mary Pickford as an orphan slave.

Pitts began working in two-reel silent comedies finding success with the slapstick scripts, audiences enjoying her characters. *Bright Eyes* in 1921 is one of her best-loved silent films, but Pitts made dozens of comedies for the studios during her first years in Hollywood. In 1921, Pitts met and married fellow actor Tom Galley; the two enjoyed successful careers and had a daughter in 1922.

It took Pitts almost ten years of hard work before she was cast in her first starring role in the 1924 film *Greed* starring Jean Hersholt and directed by Erich Von Stroheim. Stroheim stated Pitts to be one of the greatest dramatic actresses of the time when filming was complete on the ten-hour marathon motion picture. Pitts continued working with Stroheim on his next four pictures, *The Honeymoon, The Wedding March, War Nurse,* and *Walking Down Broadway,* later released under the title *Hello Sister!*

During the 1930s, Pitts worked opposite Thelma Todd on several B movies but found her niche when talking pictures changed Hollywood as the flustered, nervous worrywart in many top box office films. While enjoying her success with dramatic roles, Pitts's favorite films among fans include the comedies *Westward Passage, The Dummy, Twin Beds, No, No, Nannette,* and *The Guardsman.*

While enjoying a successful film career, Pitts went on the stage starring in Vaudeville and radio in the 1940s. Pitts worked with the top radio shows opposite Bing Crosby, Al Jolson, and Rudy Vallee. In 1944 Pitts stretched herself once again when she took a lead role in the Broadway show *Ramshackle Inn*, written specifically for her. The show was a huge success for Pitts, and she toured the country in later years, reprising her role in the play.

With the invention of television, Pitts once again strived to meet the challenge of the new medium. Pitts appeared on *G.E. True Theater, Kraft Theater, Screen Directors Playhouse*, and *The Red Skelton Hour* before landing the role, which became synonymous for the rest of her career. *The Gale Storm Show* ran for one hundred twenty-six episodes and became one of the best-loved comedies of the late 1950s. The show finally wrapped production in 1960, with Pitts coming into households as the loveable Elvira Nugent, the shipboard beautician, for five years.

Pitts suffered from declining health and was diagnosed with cancer in 1955. Even though Pitts worked through the pain of her ailments right up until the end of her life with a role in the motion pictures *The Thrill of it All* in 1963 and her final film *It's a Mad Mad Mad Mad World* in 1963. Pitts passed away on June 6, 1963, at the age of sixty-nine.

Pitts was interred at Holy Cross Memorial Park in Culver City, California, after a private service with only family in attendance.

Conclusion

The world of Hollywood has been my passion for many years, and I hope you have enjoyed reading about the great personalities that created the laughter on the silver screen.

With humble appreciation, I have been able to create this book to show another side of the people we knew through their work.

Bibliography

Books

Olen, Catherine. *The Final Curtain, Celebrity Deaths.* Atglen, Pennsylvania: Schiffer Publishing, 2010.

Chaplin, Charlie. *Charles Chaplin My Autobiography.* London, England Penguin Books Ltd, 1964.

Lloyd, Annette D'Agostino. *Harold Lloyd Magic in a Pair of Horn-Rimmed Glasses.* Albany, Georgia: BearManor Media, 2009.

Zollo, Paul. *Hollywood Remembered, An Oral History of its Golden Age.* New York, New York: Cooper Square Press, 2002.

Gehring, Wes D. *Seeing Red, The Skelton in Hollywood's Closet.* Davenport, Iowa: Robin Vincent Publishing LLC, 2001.

Keaton, Eleanor, and Vance, Jeffrey. *Buster Keaton Remembered.* New York, New York: Harry N. Abrams, Inc. 2001.

Robbins, Jhan. *Inka Dinka Doo, The Life of Jimmy Durante.* New York, New York: Paragon House, 1991.

Burns, George. *100 Years, 100 Stories.* New York, New York: G.P. Putnam's Sons, 1996.

Higham, Charles. *Lucy, The Real Life of Lucille Ball*. New York: New York, St. Martin's Press, 1986.

Basten, Fred E., and Paddy Calistro. *The Hollywood Archive, The Hidden History of Hollywood in the Golden Age*. New York, New York: Universe Publishing, 2000.

Burke, Margaret. *Final Curtain*. Santa Ana, California: Seven Locks Press, 1996.

Film and Television

A&E Biography
E! Entertainment True Hollywood Story
The Tragic Side of Comedy
The Essential Charlie Chaplin Collection
Hollywood's Classic Comedy Teams
D.W. Griffith, Years of Discovery
Jackie Gleason: Genius at Work

Internet

http://www.Hollywoodgravehunter.com
http://www.biography.com
http://www.wikipedia.com
http://www.IMDB.com
http://musicals101.com/jolson
http://nytimes.com/1982/12/07/arts/memorial-for-marty-feldman-features-laughter-and-jazz.html
http://www.filmsite.org/comedyfilms2.html
http://movies.lovetoknow.com/wiki/History_of_Comedy_Films

http://www.foxnews.com/story/0,2933,373600,00.html

http://www.eonline.com/news/richard_pryor_remem-bered_funeral/51303

http://www.johncandy.com

http://www.eonline.com/news/john_ritters_final_fare-well/45859

http://www.people.com/people/archive/arti-cle/0,,20063015,00.html

http://www.bobhope.com/bob.htm

http://www.findagrave.com

http://www.cardinalfang.net/biographies/chapman_biog.html

CPSIA information can be obtained
at www.ICGtesting.com
Printed in the USA
BVHW082252070621
608941BV00003B/529

9 781648 220180